1973

RETIREMENT
WITHOUT FEAR

RETIREMENT WITHOUT FEAR

By

LEE BUTCHER

DOW JONES BOOKS
PRINCETON, NEW JERSEY

Published by Dow Jones Books
P.O. Box 300, Princeton, NJ 08540

Printed and bound in the United States of America
10 9 8 7 6 5 4 3 2 1

Library of Congress Cataloging in Publication Data
Butcher, Lee.
  Retirement without fear.
  1. Retirement. I. Title
HQ1062.B87   301.43'5   76-17360
ISBN   0-87128-503-7

Table of Contents

Contents

Contents

Chapter 11: The Law, Swindlers and the Retiree

Keeping your affairs in order.
Mistakes can be irreparable.
Why wills are important.
Consulting a lawyer about housing.
Joint-ownership and trust agreements.
How to select a trustee.
Why retirees are targets of swindlers.
Advice on protecting yourself.

Chapter 12: Senior Power and the Future

Political power of an older population.
Senior-Citizen Intern program.
A right-to-work law for retirees?
A list of legislative proposals.
Gearing up for Gray Power.

Chapter 13: Four Success Stories

Adjustment to retirement is individual matter.
A new job for Chilly Harner.
Charles Bush's early "retirement."
New routine suits John Baxter.
New climate for Virginia Kunzic.

A Personal Note

When I told a friend in his seventies I was writing a book about retirement, he smiled and asked, "What does a 39-year-old man know about retirement?"

The question was legitimate. Yet, living in Florida, I had become familiar with many people who are dealing with the problems and promises of retirement. And I had gone through an experience that brought all the problems of retirement on me in the extreme despite my age.

At age thirty-six, a series of heart attacks caused me to leave a job as a magazine editor. The recuperative period was long and expensive. Because I retired and wasn't disabled, I had no source of income—not even Social Security. I was faced with earning a living, learning how to live on a reduced income, and adjusting my life to a much different pace.

Nevertheless, like many retirees, I was elated at first because I felt free to do what I wanted to do, not what I had to do. The elation was short-lived, as I soon found the days growing longer. Even though I was busy writing, it was in a totally different atmosphere. Previously, I was surrounded by co-workers. Now I was all alone.

The adjustment to the freedom from a set job-schedule was the most difficult thing of all. Many busy people do not take the time to develop interests outside of their work. I had been no different. And when I tried fishing, I found that one can only fish so many hours a day. Gardening soon ceased to be fun and became a dreaded chore. The things I *thought* I wanted to do were not things that held my interest.

Gradually, with the help of a patient wife, my horizons began to expand. We started doing things together—visiting friends, going to movies, sailing, playing tennis, walking on the beach, swimming or sitting around talking. Both of us developed a new perspective on life. Instead of *forcing* myself to enjoy things, I began to let my life take its own course. I have discovered that many retirees do the same thing with success.

Nothing can prepare a person for a sudden and severe illness. But had I taken the time to learn to enjoy things other than my work, to find out more about myself and to appreciate the world around me, my adjustment to "retirement" would have been much easier. My own experience underscores the maxim that no one can start preparing for retirement too soon. You can minimize the emotional, physical and financial problems of retirement by starting now to consider how well prepared you are for that milestone in your life—which may come sooner than you think.

LEE BUTCHER

Introduction

Older Americans, like everyone else, do not live by economics alone.

They also face major adjustments, many—but not all—related to the retirement process.

Not only that, but they have a right to expect satisfactions and challenges and personal growth throughout *all* their years; there should be no cutoff point on curiosity or zest for the joys of life.

As chairman of the Senate Committee on Aging, I have a high regard for the many senior Americans I have met at hearings and in hometowns.

Many lack a sound financial base,and they must struggle to pay for their electricity *and* for their prescription drugs *and* for food.

Some complain with good reason about shortcomings in Social Security and Medicare. Some tell of their fears about muggings—and worse—right in their own neighborhoods. Some say with tightlipped determination that they will not end their days in a nursing home, no matter what.

Faced by all this and more, I find it easy to agree sometimes with a handwritten sign I once saw:

"Old Age is not for Sissies."

The Senate Committee on Aging must and will continue its investigations of poverty and hardship among older Americans. And I personally will continue my efforts to assure greater security among the elderly. Congress should, for example, reform and strengthen the Supplementary Security Income program to the point that it can serve as the vehicle for ending poverty, once and for all, among older Americans. We should make Medicare a better program, capable of ending our present overdependence upon institutions. We should, and we will, untangle the complicated federal requirements for providing services to help older people live in independence.

And the Committee on Aging will do its utmost to make

the point that older people don't have to live in statistical poverty to be desperate about the cost of living. Many middle-income retirees who thought they had prepared well for their later years are also caught up in the daily struggle to make ends meet. They need added protection, including a better Social Security cost-of-living adjustment mechanism.

Focus as the Senate Committee on Aging so often must upon the woes of aging, we should not lose sight of the other precious parts of the picture about aging in the United States today.

We should not discount what older persons are doing for themselves: Organizing senior centers, volunteering for service to others, helping younger members of their families with advice and sometimes with more tangible assistance, pioneering in new forms of part-time work (often with a community-uplift motive) and providing balance and perspective to families and their communities.

As Lee Butcher, the author of this helpful book, says, there are two views of aging in this nation: one is needlessly gloomy, seeing only despair in the later years. The other sees only "golden-agers" on golf courses or in sealed-off retirement communities, living a life of frenetic leisure and little else.

Mr. Butcher says quite rightly that both views are unfortunate. Indeed, they can be damaging, because they may blind younger people—and older ones—to the realities of retired life. And in doing that, such false views practically guarantee disappointment when retirement finally does begin.

What is needed instead—as this book makes crystal-clear—is a facing up to the fact, on the part of singles and couples fairly early in their work lifetimes, that, with good luck, they will one day be elderly. Perhaps not in spirit or in physical well-being. But certainly so in years.

Given this realization, which oddly enough is so often denied subconsciously or overtly, relatively young people can begin to regard the retirement years as a gift, rather than as a penalty for leaving the work force.

They can take aggressive action to make certain that the gift is fulfilled, rather than rendered invalid.

Their plan of action definitely must include financial forecasting. Mr. Butcher provides invaluable counsel on the possibilities and pitfalls of investment planning and savings schemes. And he makes it clear that there are no sure things, either in terms of dollar yield or satisfaction. Perhaps his best advice is: "Whatever you do, be careful."

Careful about money, yes. But willing to be daring in personal goals for retirement.

Daring in developing new interests—perhaps even a second or third career, but a career on your own terms, perhaps with reduced hours or other amenities.

Daring in looking anew at your community and wondering what can be done to make it better, for *all* age groups.

Daring in what you want for you nation, and what you will do to help the nation achieve it.

And daring in reaching people in a way that perhaps was not possible during the work years, when ego and status and anxiety often get in the way of real communication.

After decades devoted to career and family, older persons may yet become the most liberated generation of all.

Perhaps one reason, for example, that Jack Benny may have reached the height of recognition among all generations in his last years was that he had proved long before that he could make us laugh and love him. And so he kept performing, not to make a living, but to practice a form of self-renewal, for him and for us. George Burns, that amazing man who could make even Jack Benny dissolve into helpless laughter, now provides the same warmth, the same sure touch that comes with experience and with mellowing.

Experience and mellowing. These are prime rewards from life. They are worth understanding. They are worth working for. They are worth the kind of action that Mr. Butcher recommends we take. We all have a stake in the challenge of retirement.

FRANK CHURCH
Chairman,
U.S. Senate Committee on Aging

Chapter 1

How to Succeed in Retirement

(By Really Trying)

"It's like being in heaven and still being alive," seventy-three-year-old Anne Jacobs says of her life at a retirement community at Deerfield Beach, Fla. "I've got my ceramics and my painting. I've even got a wonderful husband who I met here."

In Elyria, Ohio, however, George J. Ross is not so sanguine about his forced retirement at age sixty-five. "When you have good health like I do, why waste it sitting around? You'll dry up like a prune," he says. So Mr. Ross sued the city of Elyria to give him back his job as a health inspector.

Between these two extremes are the views of most Americans. A 1977 Roper poll showed, not too surprisingly, that most younger people look forward to retiring before age sixty-two. But among people who have reached sixty, only one-third would voluntarily stop working before sixty-two. The pollsters found strong opposition to mandatory retirement at sixty-five, but Roper analysts said this reflected the desire to decide one's own retirement age rather than a wish to keep on working past sixty-five.

The most crucial issue about retirement isn't surprising, either. It's money. Americans expect to need $1,000 a month to live on when they stop working, the poll showed, and just over half expect to have adequate retirement income.

1

Not so long ago, the problems of retiring and paying for retirement were almost nonexistent because few people retired. As recently as a generation ago, men and women typically worked until they died. If they became too feeble to continue working, they were either sustained by their children or relegated to the poor house.

But the retirement revolution of recent years has changed all that. Beginning with the first Social Security retirement benefits in 1940, age sixty-five became institutionalized as the time of departure from the U.S. work force. Employer pension plans added impetus to the trend. And during frequent periods of high unemployment, the government, unions and employers have introduced new incentives for workers to retire even earlier than sixty-five. The auto industry's "thirty and out" provision, for example, gives any worker retiring with thirty years on the job a pension of $650 a month.

Of course, there's another key factor in the retirement revolution—increased life expectancy. Just fifty years ago, most people didn't live long enough to retire at sixty-five. In 1920, the average life expectancy of American men was less than fifty-four years. Now, the average is seventy-two for men and nearly seventy-eight for women. People actually reaching sixty-five can expect to live an average of almost fifteen years longer.

LIVING LONGER

Longer lives, Social Security, corporate pension plans. They all add up to the so-called golden years of retirement. Yet, if the years are golden, why are so many retired Americans living so close to the poverty level?

In a recent study, the Senate Select Committee on Aging found that half of the families in the nation headed by persons over sixty-five had incomes under $7,298, less than three-fifths the median of $12,836 for all families. A full 3.2 million, or about one-sixth, of those over sixty-five lived at the poverty level as defined by the government—income of $2,730 for a single person and $3,830 for a couple as of 1976. For the rest

2

of the population, only one-tenth lived at the poverty level.

Moreover, about 25 percent of all suicides in the U.S. are committed by people over sixty-five, although this group makes up only 10 percent of the population.

Obviously, there's no guarantee that the years will be golden after you receive your gold watch. And even if you plan ahead for the retirement years, there's no guarantee that ill health or insidious inflation won't upset your plans. But the surest way to join the one out of six retired persons (some data indicate one out of four) living in poverty is to fail to plan properly for retirement.

If you haven't given much thought to retirement, even though it may be only ten or fifteen years away, you have lots of company. For many, retirement is a repugnant thought, akin to dying, so they shelve any thinking about the subject until it's too late.

A *Wall Street Journal* check with bank officials who give financial counseling to executives quoted one such adviser as saying, "Even among the fifty-year-old executives, fewer than a third have any real idea of how they will finance their retirement." The counselors all found a general lack of preparation for the problems of retirement and growing old.

A PROFILE OF PROBLEMS

One of the most extensive studies of retirement and aging was conducted by the Institute for Interdisciplinary Studies in Minneapolis. Some 194,000 Americans over sixty-five responded to its questionnaires. The results underscore the need for careful planning before retirement:

> *Living Situation*—Most retirees lived alone or with a spouse, but a "disproportionate" number lived in either retirement or nursing homes. About half owned their homes and were responsible for maintenance.

> *Financial*—Just over half of the retirees who responded said they had difficulty making ends meet. More than a third had a hard time even pay-

ing for housing. Almost two-thirds said they had no money for "little extras."

Employment—Eighteen percent were still working part time. Half of those who were working said they did so solely for financial reasons. A quarter of those unemployed said they would like to work, not only for personal satisfaction, but also to earn extra money.

Health—Twenty-five percent said they had an illness that they couldn't afford to have treated. Another 25 percent said they couldn't receive medical or dental services when needed.

Transportation—Almost a third had difficulty getting around because they had no car, were unable to drive or couldn't reach public transportation.

Legal—Fewer than 20 percent had sought legal assistance in the previous year, but most said they needed help in preparing wills or other legal documents. Six percent said they had been victims of consumer fraud.

Food—Most said they had enough money to buy the kind of food they liked.

Life Satisfaction—Seventy-eight percent said they were happy and liked the neighborhoods where they lived. But 22 percent felt unwanted, and 17 percent of these said they have nothing to live for.

NEW POLITICAL POWER

There are at least some signs that the situation may be improving. For one thing, older Americans are beginning to throw their political weight around the way youngsters did a decade ago. It is increasingly difficult for the political establishment to ignore the 23 million Americans, or more than 10 percent of the population, who are sixty-five and over. Aside from their growing numbers, they tend to vote more regularly than the rest of the population.

Their political clout is being translated into a wealth of

new governmental programs designed to ease the burdens on older Americans: Social Security benefits now are more responsive to inflationary trends, though there is still a lag in keeping up, job-training programs are preparing retirees for second careers, age discrimination on the job and compulsory retirement are forbidden up to age seventy. The Employee Retirement Income Security Act of 1974 guarantees that workers who earn pensions will actually receive them when they retire.

But much depends on the retiree himself, and how well he plans for the day when he will no longer be rushing for the 8:15 train and collecting a regular paycheck. The University of Michigan's department of gerontology conducted a survey of people who had retired before age sixty-five. It found that 75 percent of those who had planned ahead for retirement enjoyed it. Others, who had failed to plan or who had been forced to retire, were generally unhappy with their plight, and many were looking for work to help make ends meet.

The successful retirees generally had these things in common: They were free of debt, they had saved or invested some money, they had carefully considered where they wanted to live after retiring, and they had cultivated an interest in leisure activities.

With proper advance planning, you too can minimize the financial, cultural and psychological problems that often accompany retirement. The following chapters will help you consider, among other things:

- How to analyze your present financial situation and project what it will be when you retire.
- What federal programs may assist you and how to apply for them.
- Pitfalls to avoid if you are considering moving to the Sun Belt or elsewhere when you retire.
- Considerations that should go into your decision on whether to keep your house or apartment—or move to something smaller, a townhouse, condominium or a mobile home.

5

Retirement

- How to begin preparing yourself psychologically for retirement.
- How to watch your health and prepare physically for the retirement years.

Life Expectancy

Ages 65 to 75

AGES	MALE	FEMALE
65	13.4	17.5
66	12.8	16.7
67	12.2	16.0
68	11.7	15.3
69	11.2	14.6
70	10.7	13.9
71	10.2	13.2
72	9.7	12.6
73	9.2	12.0
74	8.8	11.4
75	8.4	10.8

Source: U.S. Department of Health, Education and Welfare

Chapter 2

Where the Money Goes

Between 1974 and 1977, the estimated cost of retirement living rose by an average of $130 a month, according to the Roper Organization. Americans were polled on the income they expect to need when they retire, and the median response in the latest poll was $725 a month—at today's cost of living.

Respondents were then asked, considering changes in the cost of living, how much they thought they would end up needing by the time they actually retired. Their estimated monthly needs, allowing for inflation: $1,004.

Clearly, Americans have become aware of the effects of inflation on their standards of living. Double-digit inflation, the villain of the early 1970s, may not return to haunt those living on fixed incomes, but there is every reason to believe that the cost of living will keep rising on the order of 6 percent a year.

That 6 percent rate, year after year, means that the dollar of today will buy only a little over 50 cents worth of goods and services ten years from now. And unless your nest egg keeps getting more padding as the years go by, your retirement plans will surely go awry.

Even if Social Security payments keep pace with inflation, which isn't altogether assured, they will probably continue to provide only the bare essentials. And even 6 percent inflation can seriously erode the value of other assets, such as pension-plan benefits, insurance and savings.

To assure that your retirement dreams don't become a

nightmare, you must start now to ask yourself certain questions bearing on your financial planning:

- *At what age will you retire?*
  Your decision, of course, may depend on how attractive your employer's early-retirement benefits are. And your projection at age forty may be far different from your decision at age sixty; but most Americans do dream of retiring before age sixty-two. In any case, life-expectancy data being what they are, at sixty-five you are likely to live another 15 years. And prudent planning would call for anticipating 30 years.
- *What sort of retirement would you like?*
  Most Americans, according to the Roper poll, would like part-time work after retirement, even though many of them don't expect to need the money. If you do plan such a second career, you will stand a better chance of landing a job if you start training for it now. If you plan a life of leisure, on the other hand, you have to be ready to pay for it.
- *Where will you retire?*
  Your costs of living can vary considerably depending on where you live. But 60 percent of Americans would like to stay close to where they have been living, according to the Roper poll. Most retirees, in fact, do stay in or close to their previous homes, and only about 5 percent move from the state upon retirement.
- *How much money will you need in retirement?*
  Labor Department data put the "intermediate budget" for a retired couple at $6,738 a year. By all accounts, retirement living is somewhat cheaper than living during the working years. Mortgages often are paid off, and child-rearing usually is behind. Then again, your costs will depend largely on the kind of life you plan to lead.
- *What will your retirement income be?*
  More importantly, will your retirement income cover your costs? Other chapters will discuss in more detail

such things as Social Security and pension benefits, but determining your prospective benefits is a fairly easy matter. Other sources of income, from investments and insurance, also are easy to project.

WHAT ARE YOU WORTH?

An appropriate first step in analyzing your potential retirement finances is to figure your net worth, or the surplus of your assets over your debts. Figuring your net worth each year helps you keep track of your financial progress toward retirement goals. A net-worth calculation also helps you plan your estate—however large or small—and draw up or revise your will.

A detailed inventory of your assets, including purchase dates and serial numbers of the major items, can be invaluable in case of theft or fire, not to mention the eventual settling of your estate.

Your largest asset may be your home, whether it is a house or an apartment in a cooperative or condominium. As you pay off any mortgage over the years, you build up an equity base that adds steadily to your net worth. The equity in your home can be of great value by the time you retire. You can borrow on the home in an emergency, or you can sell it and buy something cheaper, using the balance for an investment cushion.

When you figure the value of your home, you can figure in much of any investment you have made in major additions or remodeling, but be conservative because the full cost of such investments is seldom realized on resale. Depending on how long ago the additional work was done, you can probably figure on a return of 50 percent to 75 percent. The basic part of your equity is easily determined by examining your mortgage-payment statements or consulting the mortgage holder.

Bear in mind that the sale of your house would generally involve real-estate agent commissions of 6 percent or 7 percent plus closing costs that can range upwards of $2,000. Although it won't necessarily figure in your net-worth calculations, also bear in mind that if you sell your house when you or your spouse is sixty-five or older, you may qualify for a break on capital-gains taxes beyond the normal rule that exempts you from capital-gains taxes if you reinvest in a more costly residence within eighteen months. No tax is due on any profit if you sell your house for $35,000 or less (after sale expenses), and the tax on profits at higher sales prices is considerably reduced if you are over sixty-five.

In listing your other assets, try to use current market values of securities and the cash value of your life insurance. Under new federal rules, you can also learn from your employer the cash value, if any, of your pension or profit-sharing plan at a given time before retirement. Normally, you must participate in a plan for several years before you have a "vested" interest in it.

THE LIABILITY SIDE

On the liability side of your net-worth ledger, you should list the balances due on home mortgages and other loans.

The worksheets at the end of this chapter can be used to figure assets, liabilities and net worth.

Working on that basis, you can set your retirement financial goals. Depending on your present age, you can set short-term and long-term targets and adjust your budget and savings now to try to make certain the goals can be met.

As you analyze your spending habits, you can compare them with average American families in three income categories, as compiled by the Labor Department's Bureau of Labor Statistics. The chart shows how a four-member family—a man and wife, a thirteen-year-old son and an eight-year-old daughter—spent their money. The 1974 data are based on surveys the bureau conducts about once each decade, and it should be noted that many costs have since risen appreciably. Food costs, in particular, rose about one-third within three years after the survey period.

How American Families Spend

	Lower Income	Intermediate Income	Higher Income
Food All money spent for food, including grocery bills, meals at restaurants, school lunches and at work.	$2,763	$3,548	$4,453
Housing This includes furnishings, home operations, rent or mortgage payments, real estate taxes, utilities, repair, maintenance and insurance	1,758	3,236	4,900
Transportation Public transportation, cost of operating, maintaining and buying automobile	643	1,171	1,521
Clothing New and used clothing purchases, laundry, dry cleaning, repairs	759	1,085	1,589
Personal Care Beauty parlor, haircuts, toiletries, cosmetics	231	310	439
Medical Care Group life insurance and hospitalization plan, doctor, dental and eye care, medicine, major medical insurance	738	742	774
Other Family consumption This includes money spent on books, vacations, records, liquor, cigarettes, etc.	423	786	1,297
Total consumption	7,318	10,880	14,976
Miscellaneous Charitable contributions to schools, churches, life insurance, savings and investments	415	662	1,113
Social Security Tax	553	780	787
Personal Income Taxes City, state, federal	910	2,010	3,899
Total annual budget (Individual items may not equal totals because expenditures were rounded out.)	$9,198	$14,333	$20,777

11

You can also check the distribution of your expenditure against these averages for all family units in the Labor Department survey:

Housing, excluding mortgage principal...	**31.5%**
Transportation	**21.4**
Food	**20.1**
Recreation, personal care, education	**11.4**
Clothing and upkeep	**7.8**
Health Care	**6.4**
Miscellaneous	**1.4**

Whatever your spending habits are now, they are likely to change when you retire. Per capita income in the sixty-five and older group in 1975, for one thing, was $4,100, or about 5 percent below that of the population in general.

But your expenses will probably be lower, too. If you make $20,000 a year now, perhaps $6,000 of that goes for Social Security and income taxes, group life and health insurance payments and possibly a pension plan.

You won't have most of these expenses when you retire. Your Social Security income won't be taxable, and if you contributed to a corporate pension plan, the portion that you paid will be tax-free when you get it back in benefits. At sixty-five, Medicare hospital insurance will be cost-free, and the so-called medical insurance covering physicians' fees and certain other expenses will cost a basic $7.70 a month (the charge as of the end of 1977).

Moreover, your life-insurance expenses will be relatively tiny, the federal government gives you an extra income-tax exemption after sixty-five, and some states offer concessions on personal-property and real-estate taxes.

After you retire, your expenses for such things as clothing and transportation will probably diminish, too. If you needed an extra car for commuting, you can probably sell it and save on that expense. You will probably save on lunch costs as well.

But don't be deceived into thinking that retirement living is cheap. The oft-quoted rule-of-thumb that you will need only 75 percent of your preretirement income is probably overoptimistic.

In any case, you can get some idea of the costs of retirement living from the hypothetical budgets set up by Labor Department statisticians, covering three income levels, as of the fall of 1976. The costs are for couples where the husband is sixty-five or older. The shelter allowances are based on average costs for rented dwellings or owned dwellings where mortgages have been paid off.

Budgets of Retired Couples

	Lower budget	Intermediate budget	Higher budget
Total budget	$4,695	$6,738	$10,048
Total family consumption	4,493	6,333	9,281
Food	1,443	1,914	2,402
Housing	1,613	2,334	3,653
Transportation	322	629	1,161
Clothing	206	347	535
Personal care	138	202	296
Medical care	571	574	579
Other family consumption	200	332	657
Other items	202	405	767

You can also get an idea of the effects of inflation on retired couples by noting the percentage increases from the prior autumn in the government's study. As the following chart indicates, the biggest increase was for transportation costs, including public and private transportation. Medical cost increases, which were relatively small, include only the out-of-pocket expenses of the couples. Moreover, the hypothetical couples are assumed to be in reasonably good health.

One-Year Budget Rise For Retired Couple

	Budget level		
	Lower	**Intermediate**	**Higher**
Total budget	4.3%	4.2%	4.7%
Food	1.1	0.1	0.2
Housing	6.5	6.5	6.5
Transportation	8.4	9.0	9.6
Clothing	4.0	3.9	4.1
Personal care	7.8	7.4	7.6
Medical care	3.4	3.4	3.6
Other family consumption	4.7	4.7	4.6
Other items	4.1	4.1	4.2

Distribution of Consumption Expenditures per Consumer Unit, All Families, U.S., 1960–61, and 1972–73

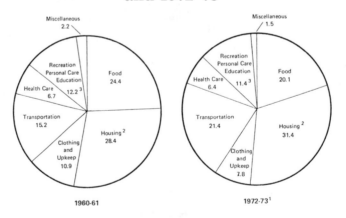

1960-61

1972-73[1]

[1] Preliminary.
[2] Excludes mortgage principal payments.
[3] Includes tobacco, alcohol, and reading.

(Source: U.S. Department of Labor, 1977)

14

Your Holdings

Assets and Liabilities	Amount
Assets:	
House..	$_____
Other real estate	_____
Life insurance...	_____
U.S. savings bonds	_____
Stocks and other bonds...	_____
Net cash value of business	_____
Automobile..	_____
Checking accounts...	_____
Savings accounts	_____
Other:	_____
....	_____
Total assets	$_____
Liabilities:	
Mortgage	$_____
Personal loans	_____
Installment loans	_____
Notes	_____
Charge accounts	_____
Other:	_____
....	_____
Total liabilities...	$_____

Your Expenses

Fixed items	Amount per month	
Rent or mortgage payment..........................	$_____	
Taxes..	_____	
Insurance	_____	
Savings..	_____	
Debt payment	_____	
Other:..	_____	
....	_____	
Total fixed.............................		$_____

Variable items

Variable items		
Food and beverages....................................	_____	
Household operation and maintenance	_____	
Furnishings and equipment.......................	_____	
Clothing	_____	
Personal	_____	
Transportation.............................	_____	
Medical care.................................	_____	
Recreation and education...........................	_____	
Gifts and contributions.............................	_____	
Other..	_____	
....	_____	
Total variable...........................		$_____
Total expenses		$_____

Chapter 3

Where the Money Comes From

In recent years, retirees in this country have seen staggering changes occur in the economy that no one, even the experts, could have predicted even a decade ago. Runaway inflation, the energy crisis and a recession, all occurring simultaneously, have made planning for tomorrow an extremely tricky business.

The shrinking dollar is the number-one problem facing anyone trying to guarantee himself a comfortable retirement. You might have your money tucked away in an ultra-safe savings account earning 5½ percent interest annually. But with inflation running at 12 to 13 percent as it did in 1974, you are actually getting a negative rate of return. You're earning nothing on your money. In fact, you're falling behind.

Arthur Levitt, comptroller of the state of New York, has said that while no one knows what the rate of inflation will be in the years to come, it is likely to remain a fact of life. And, he says, "even if it continues at 6 percent, the pensioner will be in a serious squeeze."

It's imperative, then, to start now trying to protect the buying power of your hard-earned assets.

The first rule is to have an accumulation of savings. The general rule of thumb is to keep $5,000 of savings readily available—in a passbook savings account, for example. Beyond that, you should keep perhaps a half-year's take-home pay in a similar savings plan, depending on such things as your family size and responsibilities.

The Payoff of Investing

How many years you can maintain 80% of your present standard of living in retirement if you invest 15% of your gross income:

If you begin investing 15% of your gross income at:	at an annual growth rate of:	then the column below gives the number of years after 65 your retirement fund will maintain 80% of your present standard of living if your annual income now is:			
		$15,000	$20,000	$25,000	$30,000
age 40	7%	21	16	13	13
	8%	29	21	17	16
	9%	50+	30	24	23
	10%	50+	50+	42	37
	11%	50+	50+	50+	50+
age 45	7%	15	11	10	9
	8%	18	14	12	11
	9%	25	17	15	14
	10%	40	24	19	18
	11%	50+	41	28	26
	12%	50+	50+	50+	50+
age 50	7%	10	7	6	6
	8%	11	9	7	7
	9%	14	10	9	8
	10%	17	12	10	10
	11%	22	15	12	11
	12%	37	19	15	14
	13%	50+	30	21	19
	14%	50+	50+	43	32
	15%	50+	50+	50+	50+
age 55	7%	6	4	4	4
	8%	6	5	4	4
	9%	7	5	5	4
	10%	8	6	5	5
	11%	9	7	6	5
	12%	10	7	6	6
	13%	12	8	7	7
	14%	15	10	8	8
	15%	20	12	9	9
	16%	37	15	11	10
age 60	7%	2	2	1	1
	8%	2	2	2	1
	9%	3	2	2	2
	10%	3	2	2	2
	11%	3	2	2	2
	12%	3	2	2	2
	13%	3	2	2	2
	14%	4	3	2	2
	15%	4	3	2	2
	16%	4	3	2	2

Moreover, before you consider any riskier investments, some financial counselors suggest you should have enough life insurance so that your insurance plus your savings will provide three to eight times your yearly income, depending on your expected Social Security benefits and the ages of your children.

Once you have met such rules for savings and life insurance, you can consider potentially more productive—but also riskier—ways of building a retirement nest egg.

Let's look at the various ways you can get your money to work for you.

SAVINGS ACCOUNTS

Most people start building a cash reserve with either a passbook savings account or a time deposit at a bank or savings and loan association (S&L). A passbook account requires no minimum deposit or balance, and you can withdraw or deposit funds at any time. Interest is usually paid quarterly, semi-quarterly, or yearly. Your money starts to earn interest from the day it is deposited.

Time deposits pay higher interest than passbook accounts, but you must tie up your money for a longer time, anywhere from thirty days to ten years. If you withdraw your money before the term for which you have committed it expires, you pay a penalty in the form of reduced interest, but your principal remains intact.

Both types of savings plans, whether at a commercial bank or an S&L, are insured by the government up to $40,000 for each account, giving you a high margin of safety. Unless you are already retired, however, most financial experts will advise against leaving $40,000 in such low-yield accounts.

Many retirees like to have their money in passbook or time deposits because the interest, while low, gives them a regular income that they can count on without jeopardizing their capital.

A small, regular interest payment can add up faster than you think. Suppose you saved $100 a month in an account that pays you 5½ percent interest compounded daily. In five years, your money, plus interest, would total $6,876. When you retire, a bank officer explains, you would be able to withdraw $130 each month for five years before your account was depleted. You could stretch this out for ten years, receiving $73 per month.

Or, if you chose, you could take the $6,876 and invest it in a certificate of deposit for six years or more at a savings and loan institution. If you invested it at 7¾ percent interest compounded daily, it would pay annual interest of $554 with the principal remaining intact. A bank or savings and loan association officer can give more information about the specific savings plans they offer.

Some experts advise that, no matter what your investment strategy may be, you should have an amount equal to at least four months' after-tax income set aside in savings that can be immediately convertible to cash. Once you have that much money reserved for emergencies, you can look around for higher-yielding investments for the rest of your money.

The maximum interest that banks or S&Ls can pay is established by law, and rates fluctuate with economic conditions. Each institution can set its own minimum deposit requirements on most accounts.

In recent years, passbook savings accounts have been paying a maximum annual interest of slightly over 5 percent. Savings certificates, usually offered in denominations of $1,000, pay higher interest rates, but the money must remain for a specified number of years for the higher interest rate to apply. For six-year and longer certificates, the interest rates have exceeded 8 percent.

U.S. SAVINGS BONDS

Although the rate of return on savings bonds compares unfavorably with other forms of long-term savings, they are attractive to many people because they are considered safe and convenient to buy and can be purchased in small amounts.

Series E Bonds are sold for 75 percent of their face value and can be redeemed for the face value in five years. The interest rate is 6 percent when they are held to maturity. However, the interest rate is less if you cash them in before maturity—4.54 percent at the end of the first year, for example. The smallest denomination costs $18.75 and pays $25 after five years; the largest costs $7,500 and repays $10,000 at maturity.

Series H Bonds are sold at full face value and pay interest semiannually. They return 6 percent when held to maturity of ten years. As with E bonds, the interest rate is low the first year and gradually increases until, at maturity, the bonds have returned 6 percent a year over the life of the bond. H bonds are sold in denominations of $500 to $10,000.

Each year, Americans invest billions of dollars in U.S. Savings Bonds, partly because they are so easy to purchase. A Series E bond can be bought through a payroll savings plan for as little as $1.25 a week. The money is automatically deducted from a paycheck before it reaches the employee, eliminating the temptation to spend it for other things. Banks also offer a "bond a month" program, where funds are automatically deducted from accounts to purchase E Bonds.

Periodically, the interest rates are increased on U.S. Savings Bonds. The current 6 percent rate was established in 1973. All outstanding E and H bonds are still earning interest. A single person is permitted to buy up to $10,000 a year face value in either bond; a couple can purchase bonds up to $20,000 face value annually. If the bonds are lost, stolen or destroyed, they will be replaced by the U.S. Treasury at no cost. Should you lose a bond, write to the Bureau of Public Debt, P.O. Box 509, Parkersburg, W. Va., 26101, to have it replaced.

Interest on savings bonds is exempt from state and local income taxes, but it is subject to federal income tax. The federal tax on Series E bond interest can be deferred until the bonds are redeemed. Income tax on H bond interest must be paid each year.

Federal income tax on E bonds can be avoided if they are converted to H bonds. Many retirees do this so they can defer income taxes until later, lower-income years.

One investor started buying a Series E bond each month, paying $37.50 for a bond of $50 face value. He expects to buy a bond a month for the next fifteen years. At the end of that time, he will have bonds worth $10,699, which includes nearly $4,000 in interest that he hasn't had to pay income taxes on. After 15 years, he intends to convert the E bonds for $11,000 worth of Series H bonds by adding $301 out of his own pocket. He will have avoided income taxes on the E bonds completely and begin receiving regular interest payments after he retires, when his income (and tax rate) will be lower. This is a favorite method of building retirement income by people who have limited earning power.

LIFE INSURANCE

The purpose of life insurance can be two-fold. All life insurance provides money for your family if you die, and certain types of life insurance also offer a method of saving. You should know, however, that you can't have it both ways on the "saving" type. If you keep the policy until you die and your family collects the insurance, the underlying savings plan, or "cash value" of the policy, becomes irrelevant. Conversely, if you wish to cash in your policy during your lifetime to take advantage of your accumulated savings, the insurance protection is canceled.

A stockbroker, who believes life insurance is a poor way to save money, also admits it may be one way an undisciplined money manager can build up capital.

"The one sure thing that life insurance does is force somebody to save," the broker says, "You can put your money to better use in other investments, but almost everybody thinks life insurance is absolutely essential."

Not all types of coverage offer a savings option, however. *Term insurance buys nothing but protection. It pays death benefits to your family if you die during the term the policy covers, usually five, ten or twenty years. Your premiums rise steadily as you grow older and you renew your policy at the end of each term.*

Whole, or straight, life insurance protects your family in case of death and at the same time allows you to build up savings. Unlike term insurance, whole life never expires, and the premiums always remain the same. You may cash in the policy at any time, but in such cases you normally receive less than the face value of the policy. You can also borrow at a low rate of interest—usually 5 to 6 percent a year—against the cash value of your whole life insurance.

Term insurance premiums are roughly half those of whole life, and for young people term insurance represents a good way of getting protection at a relatively low cost.

Endowment insurance is by far the most expensive. It also combines insurance and savings, but as the premiums are higher, your equity accumulates faster. If the insured dies, the beneficiary gets the face value of the policy, but if the insured lives to the maturity date he gets the face value—his accumulated savings—in a lump sum, and the insurance is canceled.

How much insurance do you need? Some experts recommend that you should have insurance equal to five times your annual salary. But the amount varies widely depending on your family's needs. Before you try to calculate, consider questions like these: Does your wife have marketable job skills that would enable her to earn some income if you died? How much would your family receive in Social Security survivor's benefits if you should die? Have you provided for your children's education? What are your debts and financial obligations?

For an investor at age thirty-eight, here are some insurance programs we investigated and how they worked out as savings programs. The monthly premium for a $25,000 whole life insurance policy was $41.47 a month. At the end of five years, the insured person would have paid $2,231.25, but it would have a guaranteed cash value of only $1,200. If he elected to convert it to a paid-up policy, the insurance protection would be $3,125.

At the end of the 20-year life of the policy, he would have paid $8,925 and the cash value would be $8,100. The paid-up policy would insure him for $14,350. There would be no further payments after 20 years and, at age sixty-five, he could cash the policy for $11,500 or elect to receive $71.60 a month for ten years. The protection would be canceled immediately if the policy was converted to cash, or in ten years if the monthly payments were received.

Term insurance at $91 per year offered $17,300 against loss of life for the first year and decreased to $5,560 at the end of ten years. The difference in the term and whole life insurance premiums was $355.20 a year. Investing that amount in Series E bonds for 20 years would accumulate bonds worth $9,472, which is $2,208 less than the guaranteed cash value of the $25,000 whole life insurance policy.

By all means, shop around when buying insurance. Premiums for similar coverage vary markedly from company to company. A Pennsylvania Insurance Department survey found that one company charged nearly three times as much for virtually the same coverage offered by a competitor.

Before consulting an insurance agent, have a clear idea of what you need and want. Herbert S. Denenberg, former Commissioner of Insurance for Pennsylvania, says, "You'd better know enough about it to buy the product intelligently—or it will be rammed down your throat."

Once you have established your emergency reserve in a risk-free savings plan and have satisfied yourself that your insurance coverage is adequate, you are ready to try to make your nest egg grow.

Before we deal with the individual types of investments available to you, we should note some cautions offered by financial advisers:

    —Look before you leap. Before choosing a brokerage house, find out what investments they have recommended to investors in the past. Check how well these securities have performed by consulting the financial pages of old newspapers in the library. Alternatively, make some hypothetical investments based on a brokers recommendations, and wait a few months or more to see how well the choices would have worked out. All of this will provide no guarantee, but it will provide a basis for judgment.

—Don't take at face value everything the broker tells you. Many brokers are highly reputable professionals, and they are more apt to keep your business if they do well by you. But their main function (and main source of income) is in selling securities. They can make costly mistakes—with *your* money.

—Once you have made an investment, keep abreast of this investment in particular and economic trends in general. Keep an eye out for developments that could affect your investments.

COMMON STOCK

When you buy a share of common stock, you are buying a share of the ownership in a corporation. You usually expect to make money two ways—through dividend payments the company makes to shareholders and through appreciation in the price of the stock.

Shares of most well-established companies pay quarterly dividends. But even at the depressed prices of most stocks in recent years, the dividend rates are typically lower than the investor could earn in a good savings plan or in the relatively safe bond market.

So capital appreciation is what most investors seek in the stock market. If a company prospers, and its stock price increases, the investor benefits.

Traditionally, the stock market has been a hedge against inflation, but in the past ten years or so, as inflation has continued and occasionally spurted, common stocks have not only failed to keep pace with inflation, they have barely held their own. Even the blue-chip stocks represented by the Dow

Jones industrial average were just about at the same levels in 1977 as they were in 1967. This performance would clearly represent a disaster for a retiree who had no other investments at a time of continuing inflation.

PREFERRED STOCK

Some companies, besides raising capital by selling common stock, also issue "preferred stock." Holders of preferred stock are given preference when dividends are handed out. If profits go down and the dividend has to be cut, the dividend on the common stock is first to go. In rare cases, the preferred stock dividend may be cut, too. But if profits go up again, preferred holders have the right to receive all their overdue dividends before a dividend can be paid on the common stock.

Preferred stock is a good way of getting a steady cash income. But it has a disadvantage: Your dividends never change. Even if the company's profits suddenly spurt upward, causing management to raise the common dividend, preferred dividends remain the same.

BONDS

When you buy a bond, you essentially are lending a corporation or municipality money for which you are paid a fixed rate of interest. Bonds are issued for a specified period of time, often twenty years or more. When they mature after that period, you get back the face amount of the bond. A high-quality corporate bond is usually a good, safe investment. Some currently pay annual interest of 8 to 9 percent.

Be aware of the disadvantages however: Bonds must be bought in large denominations—$1,000 is usually the bare minimum. Bond prices fluctuate on the open market, in response to ups and downs in interest rates. If prices decline, you may have to wait until the maturity date to get back the face amount of the bond.

Before investing in bonds, get expert advice. Although good-quality bonds and notes are a less risky investment than most common stocks, they are by no means foolproof, as over

100,000 small investors in New York City issues learned in 1975. The city, laboring under an astronomical operating deficit, announced a "debt moratorium," which meant that holders weren't able to redeem certain notes coming due. Instead, they were asked to exchange the securities for other notes with longer terms and lower interest rates.

MUTUAL FUNDS

Over seven million Americans choose to put their investment money into mutual funds. Most of them do so because they have neither the time nor the talent to keep tabs on the gyrations of the stock market, nor the cash to plan a diversified investment program. One investment adviser says that unless you have a minimum of $25,000 to put into the stock market and the time to watch a series of diversified investments, you are better off in a mutual fund.

Mutual funds are investment companies that pool the assets of a large number of investors to buy stocks. Your money is automatically invested in a wide variety of stocks and bonds, and it is managed by professionals.

But a fund is only as good as the people who manage it, and in recent years, mutual funds haven't always provided a respectable rate of return for those who invested in them.

"I watched the market steadily decline and decided to sell and buy into mutual funds for protection," one investor complained. "It was like jumping out of the frying pan into the fire."

Mutual funds began to lose money in 1974, as the stock market plunged and investors by the thousands began trying to salvage as much of their money as they could. Investment Company Institute, an industry trade group, reported that shareholders withdrew over $289 million more than they invested in mutual funds in 1974. And for 1975, that withdrawal figure rose to $10.1 billion.

Lipper Analytic Services, which keeps track of the performance of more than 500 funds, reported that in 1974, the mutual fund industry average dropped 22.57 points, almost as steep a decline as the Dow Jones industrial average, which slumped 27.58 points. More recently, the mutual funds have been doing better. In the first nine months of 1977, for example, Lipper says 477 funds averaged a decline of just 0.29 percent, while the Dow Jones industrial average plunged 15.68 percent.

Study a fund's prospectus and latest financial statements to determine its financial position, its investment philosophy and performance record over the past year.

Open-End Funds and Closed-End Funds—Open-end mutual funds set no limit on the number of shares they sell to the public. If you invest in this type of fund, you can always quickly convert your shares to cash by selling them back to the fund. The price is determined by the fund's market value at the time.

A closed-end investment company neither issues new shares nor buys back existing ones. It issues only a fixed number of shares that are then traded back and forth among investors like stock in General Motors or any other publicly held company. The value fluctuates just like that of any other stock.

Load and No-Load Funds—When you buy into a mutual fund, you aren't getting its professional management service free. You pay a small fee for having your money managed by professionals.

In addition, if you buy what is known as a load fund, you have to pay an 8½ percent commission on the first year's purchases at the time of sale to the selling agent. What's more, if you reinvest your gains, as most people do, the broker charges an additional 8½ percent commission for that service. About 70 percent of the mutual funds sold are load funds, purchased through brokers.

No-load funds, on the other hand, charge no sales fee. But because brokers don't get commission on this type of order, you have to locate them yourself. This isn't difficult. The financial pages of your newspaper list mutual-fund quotations. Those marked with an NL are no-load.

You can obtain a prospectus by writing to the fund itself. Financial advisers suggest you look for a fund that has recorded realized capital gains over a ten-year period and hasn't had more than a year or so of declines greater than those of the Dow Jones industrial average in that period.

More information on no-load funds can be obtained from the No-Load Mutual Fund Association, Valley Forge Colony Building, Valley Forge, Pa., 19481. But purchases of the shares of no-load funds are made through the funds themselves.

MUNICIPAL BOND FUNDS AND UNIT TRUSTS

Relatively safe investments like bank savings accounts and government and corporate bonds are considered "defensive" investments. Another so-called defensive investment is the municipal bond, issued by cities, states and other municipalities, although those who invested in the New York City issues discovered a couple of years ago that they aren't always so safe. The big advantage to municipals is that they are exempt from federal tax and from tax in the city and state where they are issued.

Two popular ways for individuals to invest in municipal bonds in increments as low as $1,000 have emerged in recent years—municipal bond mutual funds, first allowed under a 1976 law, and unit trusts. Both systems allow the investor to reduce the risk because the underlying investment is spread among many states and municipalities.

With the unit trust, investors buy a stake in 25 or more issues. The units, which come due in twenty to thirty years as a rule, are sold by major brokerage firms, which charge sales commissions of about 3 percent to 4.5 percent.

Shares in the bond mutual funds involve a similar commission, or "load," if they are bought through a broker. But there are some funds—Fidelity Municipal Bond Fund and Dreyfus Tax Exempt Bond Fund, to name two of the largest—that are bought directly and therefore involve no commission.

The unit trusts pay a slightly higher rate of interest in

general (over 6 percent, tax free, in late 1977). But unless you are prepared to keep your money invested for the 20 or 30 years until the issues mature, you probably should invest in the managed funds rather than the unit trusts.

The holder of a unit trust who is forced to sell faces a sales charge as high as 4.5 percent, and the investment firm sponsoring the unit trust, which generally will buy back your units if you wish to sell, may put a lower value on your shares than you expect. Check the prospectus for the method of evaluation in the event of such a repurchase.

The managed funds, on the other hand, generally impose no sales charges, making their commissions instead by charging management fees of about 0.5 percent of assets a year.

Not only is selling your interest easier in the municipal bond fund, but you can more easily keep track of the value of your investment, because newspapers like *The Wall Street Journal* each day quote the net asset values—representing the approximate purchase and sale price. With the unit trust, you get an annual accounting only.

REAL ESTATE

Home ownership has historically been one of the safest hedges against inflation. While many stocks have fluctuated in value, the price of the average home has been steadily increasing. The U.S. Department of Housing and Urban Development reported that the average selling price of a home— whether old or new—increased 15 percent during 1975. The stability of this investment, coupled with the tax advantages of holding a mortgage during high-earning years, has led most financial advisers to recommend home ownership as the cornerstone of a family's investment strategy.

What, specifically, are the advantages of home ownership? When you buy a home, you start building equity that accrues throughout the life of the mortgage. Thus you are paying your housing expenses and investing at the same time. Moreover, tax laws favor the buyer: You can deduct mortgage interest and real estate taxes from your federal income tax.

And usually, the home buyer will be able to sell the home for more than he paid for it or borrow against it in later years.

Renters, by contrast, have nothing to show for their monthly housing expenses. They build no equity and have no tax advantages.

Building equity in a home can be particularly important in planning for retirement. If you have arranged to pay off your mortgage by the time you retire, you'll be able to live rent-free—an advantage that the lifetime renter won't have.

As attractive as home ownership may be, it isn't that easy in today's economy. In mid-1978, the selling price of a single-family home was $53,500—well beyond the means of many young families. The housing industry has begun to offer more affordable housing in the form of multifamily condominiums and, more recently, "no-frills" houses that are similar to the basic homes constructed after World War II when demand for housing was high and buyers were less affluent. Whether you choose a home, a condominium or a new no-frills house, by owning rather than renting, you enjoy significant tax advantages while investing in your future.

How much should you spend on a home? Fay T. Plowman, a housing specialist with the U.S. Department of Agriculture, recommends that to start with, you forget some of the familiar rules of thumb, such as the warning to spend no more than 2½ times your annual income. Since each family's financial circumstances are different, such formulas are meaningless, she says. It's far better, she adds, to take a close look at your own budget. See what you spend on non-housing expenses and subtract these from your net pay. The difference should give you a good idea of what you can afford for housing. Be sure to figure into your housing budget the considerable cost of upkeep.

"Although monthly payments on a mortgage should be as large as possible," Ms. Plowman says, "a family needs to guard against getting in too deep. Home ownership should not be undertaken at the expense of other joys of family living."

31

THOUGHTS ON INVESTING

When you are younger and in your peak earning years, you should be investing to build equity. But when you retire, the rainy day you've been saving for has arrived. Instead of continuing to try to build equity, you should be more concerned with ways to increase your income. Usually that's done by switching from growth stocks to safer investments that provide a steady income.

For example, a paid-up mutual fund can be turned into an annuity paying a fixed income. Low-yield growth stocks might be sold and converted into Series H savings bonds, paying a guaranteed interest rate. If you sell stock after you've retired, you should consult a lawyer or accountant to enable you to take advantage of any capital-gains tax breaks for which you may be eligible.

Some retirees are so concerned about leaving an estate that they resist converting their equity into income-producing investments. But unless you are wealthy, this can be unwise.

"There's too much emphasis on estate planning," a writer nearing retirement age says. "People scrimp and save and deprive themselves so they can leave some money to ungrateful children who won't even appreciate it."

This assessment may sound bitter, but it is echoed by many people who know the problems of retirees first-hand. A retired sociologist in Miami puts it another way: "Take care of yourself first, even though you may love your children dearly. After all, you're the one who can't get out and earn money."

YOU DON'T HAVE TO BE RICH

You don't have to make a six-digit salary to build the resources necessary to protect yourself in retirement, as the following example shows.

Money magazine found a Midwesterner who had built up a net worth of more than $200,000 on a salary that has never exceeded $15,000 a year. The shrewd money manager is Rex

Reynolds, a sales manager for an Effingham, Ill., fuel-distribution firm, who now earns a salary of $10,000 a year. Reynolds expects to retire at age sixty-two with an annual income of $24,000, or slightly less than he earns now from his salary and investments.

Mr. Reynolds concedes that he and his wife could get by on less, perhaps, but "fear of the unknown" has prompted him to aim for the $24,000 retirement-income goal. He seems likely to achieve his goal, because both he and his wife have been careful with their money all their lives.

Throughout their married life, Mr. Reynolds says, not a month has gone by when they haven't saved money—"even if it was only a dollar." They haven't deprived themselves in the process, but they live within their means. If they want something they can't afford immediately, they save for it.

Mr. Reynolds worked nineteen years as a middle-level executive for a major oil company. He was terminated at age 50, during a labor cutback, when he was making $15,000 a year. Each of those nineteen years, he had put 10 percent of his paycheck into a company thrift plan. When he left, he was able to withdraw $67,000 including interest. He also had been buying company stocks and sold these for a profit of $7,500.

On his peak salary of $15,000, Mr. Reynolds had amassed:

Assets:

stocks	$84,011
mutual funds	35,166
house	34,000
bonds	21,050
land	18,500
cash life insurance	15,000
furniture, personal effects	8,500
automobile	2,650
checking account	1,913
	$220,790

Liabilities:

mortgage	$ 11,700
life insurance loans	5,350
bank loan	500
	$17,550

Total Net Worth: $203,240

A look at Mr. Reynolds' balance sheet reveals that he has followed the rules of prudent financial management: He has protected his family with life insurance, invested in both equity stocks and income-producing instruments. He has diversified his investments, and has assets that can be converted into income when he retires.

An impressive accomplishment, perhaps, but nothing that any frugal and foresighted individual couldn't match provided he started early enough building financial security for retirement.

BUT IF YOU ARE RICH...

Some guidelines for investors who have already accumulated substantial nest eggs were presented in a *Wall Street Journal* analysis by Charles M. Eckman, a professional financial counselor at Oakland Financial Group in Charlottesville, Va.

Eckman's profiles of five investors assumed they had at least $100,000 in funds available for investment. The major investment goals were diversification and hedging against inflation.

HIGH-INCOME EXECUTIVE, Age 45

Checking and savings accounts: 5%.
Precious metals (gold stocks or gold, as examples): 15%.
Leveraged mortgaged real estate: 20%.
Capital shares in "dual" mutual funds: 15%.
Municipal bond fund (15% long-term, 10% short-term): 25%.
Growth stocks: 20%.

The real-estate investment excludes the executive's equity in his own home. "Dual" mutual funds are funds that divide their portfolios between capital-growth investments and income investments; owners of "capital" shares receive capital gains of the entire portfolio, while owners of "income" shares receive dividend income from the entire portfolio.

JUNIOR EXECUTIVE, Age 32

Checking and savings accounts: 5%.
Precious metals: 20%.
Discounted convertible bonds: 20%.
Leveraged real estate: 25%.
Growth stocks: 20%.
Put and call options: 10%.

PROFESSIONAL, Age 35 With Two Children

Checking and savings accounts: 10%.
Short-term education trusts, half invested in convertible bonds, half in convertible preferred stocks: 30%.
Precious metals: 20%.
Capital shares in dual funds: 20%.
Single-premium deferred annuity: 20%.

RETIRED EXECUTIVE

Checking and savings accounts: 5%.
Money-market fund: 20%.
Corporate or utility bonds, A-rated or better, with maturities staggered from two years to 20 years: 50%
Blue-chip income stocks: 25%.

MIDDLE-AGED WIDOW

Checking and savings accounts: 5%.
Money-market fund: 15%.
Precious metals: 10%.
Shares of American Telephone & Telegraph: 10%.
Short-term U.S. Treasury bonds: 10%.
Corporate bond funds: 25%.
No-load mutual funds: 25%.

Retirement

In the widow's case, Eckman suggests AT&T for its relative safety and liquidity and its earnings history, and also because he believes an aging widow will be psychologically comfortable holding it. For investors who fear the government's antitrust attack on AT&T, or who are reluctant to buy its shares for other reasons, he suggests General Telephone & Electronics.

Chapter 4

Social Security And You

If you are one of the 100 million people paying into the Social Security system through payroll taxes, you have a right to wonder whether you will eventually receive your just returns.

Developments of recent years, at least, have cast some doubt on the long-term viability of the system, which in earlier years was accumulating surpluses. In the first decades after the first benefits were paid in 1940, the Social Security system was generally taking in more revenues from payroll taxes than it was distributing in benefits, at times building up a trust fund of as much as $50 billion.

But in 1975, benefit payments exceeded incoming revenues by $2.7 billion, and there was talk of tapping general tax revenues to sustain the program. As the deficits continued, Commerce Secretary Juanita Kreps in 1977 even suggested that Social Security benefits begin at age sixty-eight instead of sixty-five—bringing an outcry from those who considered this a fraud on people planning for years to retire at sixty-five.

While Congress is unlikely to let the Social Security system come apart at the seams, the deficits seem certain to continue—and even increase—without substantial new revenues. For one thing, recent declines in the birth rate will mean fewer taxpayers to help pay the benefits of those born in the "baby boom" years after World War II.

Just now, about 30 retired Social Security recipients are covered for each 100 working taxpayers contributing to the program, but the number probably will be 48 retirees for each 100 workers by the year 2030, the Census Bureau says.

Social Security is a system of social insurance in which employees, employers and self-employed workers contribute during their working years to insure the employees and their families against loss of earnings through retirement, disability or death.

The system actually consists of three separate programs providing retirement and survivor benefits, payments to the disabled and health insurance for the aged, known as Medicare. The programs are financed by separate trust funds, fed mainly by the payroll tax levied on a maximum of $17,700 annual earnings (starting in 1978) for each worker enrolled. The tax rate has gone up steadily over the years, along with benefits, and the advent of Medicare benefits in 1966, sped the ascent.

Employer and employee each pays a tax of 6.05 percent, and this is scheduled to rise progressively to 7.15 percent in 1986. For employees earning at least $17,700 in 1978, the tax was $1,070.85, levied on both employee and employer. Benefits have been rising too, as we shall see, and now are linked to increases in the cost of living.

"In one way or another, Social Security touches the lives of nearly every American," says James B. Cardwell, commissioner of the Social Security Administration. "Nine out of ten jobs are covered. More than 32 million people—retired and disabled workers and their dependents and the dependent survivors of deceased workers—receive Social Security cash benefits."

Obviously, Social Security has become more than a huge government pension plan. Yet for most Americans, the pension is the program's most important function.

WHO QUALIFIES?

To qualify for Social Security, you must have credit for a certain amount of work while paying Social Security taxes, and the amount of your benefits will depend on your average earnings over a period of years.

Whether you take full benefits at 65 or reduced benefits sometime after reaching 62, your spouse will receive an additional monthly payment. If both the worker and his spouse are 65, for example, the additional payment for the spouse will be half the worker's own benefit.

For each three-month calendar quarter that you work under Social Security and are paid $50 or more, you get credit for one quarter. The following tables, provided by the Social Security Administration, show how much credit is needed for retirement and survivors' benefits.

Under a special rule, cash payments can be made to a worker's children and their mother or father even though the worker dies with fewer credits than normally required, provided he or she has worked under Social Security one-and-a-half years in the three years before death.

Benefits from Social Security aren't automatic; you must apply for them. Many widows have gone for many months without receiving benefits when their husbands died because they didn't realize they had to apply—even for the lump-sum payment of $255 made at a worker's death. A court ruling

Work credit for retirement benefits

If you reach 62 in	Years you need
1975	6
1976	6¼
1977	6½
1978	6¾
1979	7
1981	7½
1983	8
1987	9
1991 or later	10

Work credit for survivors' benefits

Born after 1929, die at	Born before 1930, die before age 62	Years you need
28 or younger		1½
30		2
32		2½
34		3
36		3½
38		4
40		4½
42		5
44		5½
46	1975	6
47	1976	6¼
48	1977	6½
50	1979	7
52	1981	7½
54	1983	8
56	1985	8½
58	1987	9
60	1989	9½
62 or older	1991 or later	10

against a widow in 1975 said that "ignorance is no excuse" for failing to apply.

To estimate your eventual Social Security benefits, ask at any Social Security office for a leaflet, "Estimating Your Social Security Retirement Check." The Social Security Administration also provides these guidelines:

Examples of monthly Social Security payments (effective June 1976)

	Average yearly earnings after 1950				
Benefits can be paid to a:	$923 or less	$3,000	$5,000	$8,000°	$10,000°
Retired worker at 65	107.90	223.20	304.50	427.80	474.00
Worker under 65 and disabled	107.90	223.20	304.50	427.80	474.00
Retired worker at 62	86.40	178.60	243.60	342.30	379.20
Wife or dependent husband at 65	54.00	111.60	152.30	213.90	237.00
Wife or dependent husband at 62	40.50	83.70	114.30	160.50	177.80
Wife under 65 and one child in her care	54.00	118.00	257.40	321.00	355.60
Widow or dependent widower at 65 (if worker never received reduced benefits)	107.90	223.20	304.50	427.80	474.00
Widow or dependent widower at 60 (if sole survivor)	77.20	159.60	217.80	305.90	339.00
Widow or dependent widower at 50 and disabled (if sole survivor)	56.80	111.70	152.40	214.00	237.10
Widow or widower caring for one child	161.90	334.80	456.80	641.80	711.00
Maximum family payment	**161.90**	**341.20**	**561.90**	**748.70**	**829.50**

*Maximum earnings covered by Social Security were lower in past years and must be included in figuring your average earnings. This average determines your payment amount. Because of this, amounts shown in the last two columns generally won't be payable until future years. The maximum retirement benefit generally payable to a worker who is 65 in 1977 is $412.70.

Beginning with 1978, you can earn as much as $4,000 a year without having any benefits withheld if you are between sixty-five and seventy-two. Under the 1977 Social Security legislation, the limit will rise to $4,500 in 1979, to $5,000 in 1980 and to $5,500 in 1981. In 1982, the age at which Social Security beneficiaries will no longer be subject to an earnings limit will drop to seventy from seventy-two, while the limit for those sixty-five to seventy will rise to $6,500. The new law eliminated an earlier provision that allowed benefits to be paid for months of low earnings regardless of annual earnings.

EARLY RETIREMENT

About half the men and about two-thirds of the women who apply for Social Security retirement benefits nowadays are below the age of sixty-five. Both men and women can apply as early as age sixty-two, but at sixty-two they receive benefits 20 percent lower than the age-sixty-five benefits— and this reduced rate continues throughout the retirement. If you retire after age sixty-two but before age sixty-five, benefits are reduced by five-ninths of one percent for each month before sixty-five that you retire.

If you change your mind and return to work after you start getting retirement checks, your added earnings will often result in higher benefits when you stop working again.

Retirement before age sixty-two has been made an attractive proposition in a number of labor contracts in recent years, partly as a way to reduce unemployment among younger workers in some industries. But before you elect such an option, be sure to check on the effect this will have on your eventual Social Security benefits at age sixty-two or later.

NEED FOR OTHER INCOME

The current maximum Social Security payment of $474 a month is a far cry from the $22.54 paid to the first recipient in 1940, and benefits now are raised automatically after the cost of living index climbs at an annual rate of more than 3 percent. But the 1976 average benefits of $2,600 paid to single recipients represented income barely above the poverty level for elderly persons.

Many elderly people who retired when private pension plans were either nonexistent or not guaranteed are painfully aware of how inadequate Social Security benefits can be if they aren't supplemented by other income. This is particularly true of those who worked when wages were much lower, since their Social Security benefits are related to income levels when they were still employed.

One man, testifying before the House Select Committee on Aging, noted that he had worked during the Depression years, sometimes earning no more than 50 cents a day, and as a result he hadn't been able to contribute much to the Social Security fund in those years (payments into Social Security began in 1935). Now, he said, when a loaf of bread costs more than a day's wages did back then, he is hard-pressed to get by on his meager benefits.

DEATH AND DISABILITY

Social Security offers a wage earner and his family financial protection before he retires in cases of his death or disability. The insurance against loss of earnings is an important consideration for people who are still working, because it can influence how much disability and life insurance they buy.

Consider this example of a thirty-four-year-old married man with two children, who was earning $15,700 a year when he was killed in an automobile accident in 1976. Because he was eligible for maximum survivors' benefits at the time, his widow and children began receiving $718 a month from Social Security, or more than $8,600 a year, tax-free.

By the time his oldest child reaches eighteen, the family will have received more than $112,000, not counting increases in benefit levels in the meantime. At age sixty, his widow would begin receiving monthly retirement benefits, unless she has remarried. His children could keep receiving payments until age twenty-two if they remain in school.

A worker is also protected against loss of income if he becomes disabled. Whereas six years of Social Security coverage are needed to be eligible for retirement benefits, fewer years and higher earnings levels are used to figure the average earnings for young workers. So disability and survivors' benefits reach higher levels more quickly when benefits are increased. A man disabled in 1977 at age twenty-nine or younger and with average covered yearly earnings of $14,700 over two years, for example, would receive a disability benefit of almost $567 a month.

SPECIAL PROBLEMS

In 1972, Congress passed a law that created the Supplemental Security Income (SSI) program, which provides cash grants to the nation's aged, blind and disabled poor.

Depending on the state of residence and on the recipient's financial need, the SSI payments range up to $157.70 per month for an individual and $236.80 per month for a couple.

There are rigid requirements that must be met before one can receive SSI. The law allows an individual to have no more than $1,500 in assets, excluding his home if it is valued under $25,000. Household goods, a car worth $1,200 or less and a life insurance policy with a cash value of under $1,500 are also excluded. Total assets for a couple can be no more than $2,250.

Some feel these restrictions are too stringent. One man told a congressional committee: "We want to be able to pay our own funeral expenses. So we have $2,500 set aside . . . that we never touch because we want to go out without being a burden to anyone. But it keeps us from receiving the Supplemental Security Income."

At a hearing before a subcommittee of the House Select Committee on Aging in Iowa, Mrs. Hallie Shaffer, an elderly retiree, presented a budget sheet that she said she hoped would show "the almost impossible task an elderly couple has in this country today in meeting our financial responsibilities on a month-to-month basis."

Mrs. Shaffer said that she and her husband receive a combined monthly Social Security income of $348.60. Their only other asset is a savings account, which at the time of her testimony contained $2,394.94.

She presented the following list of monthly expenses:

Rent	$30.00
Food Stamps	38.00
Other groceries	125.00
Blue Cross/Blue Shield	56.00*
Electricity	12.37
Gas	5.79
Water	10.14
Phone	8.15
Soap, aspirin	6.60
TV repair	8.81

*-Quarterly payment.

In addition, she said her husband, who suffers from a serious heart condition, requires medication that costs about $65 a month. Cab fare to and from doctor's appointments totals about $5 a month. In July, her husband's hearing aid needed repair, at a cost of $6. Counting miscellaneous items, their total expenses that month were $421.37.

Noting that their expenses continually exceed their income, Mrs. Shaffer said: "The only way we are able to meet our monthly expenses is to continuously dip into our savings account to make up the difference."

She said they have applied for both SSI and Medicaid but have been turned down because their assets were considered too high. "I don't think we are in any way living too elaborately or are asking for more than we need," she said. "All we really ask is to live and die, when that time comes, with dignity."

PENALTIES FOR WORKING

Not only are your Social Security benefits reduced when you earn more than $3,000 a year after retirement, but your wages are subject to federal taxes, including Social Security tax.

"We aren't supposed to give people advice on whether to work or not," explained a frustrated Social Security office manager, "but it is just ridiculous for a retired person to go out and get a job. They need money so desperately and, when they earn it, the Social Security Administration takes it away from them."

The director of a senior-citizens organization says the work penalties are "confiscatory" and lead to "widespread nonreporting of income by persons who have never knowingly violated a law." He says the rule also "virtually forces retirement and its companion loss of purpose in life."

Social Security law is inconsistent when it comes to income after retirement, for a person receiving Social Security can earn dividends on investments in unlimited amounts without having his benefit reduced. It is only when an employer-employee relationship exists that Social Security is reduced.

"It is ridiculous to set up roadblocks to working as we grow older," says one critic of the system, "and then complain about the cost of providing for an ever-increasing nonworking population."

WOMEN'S BENEFITS

Women who hold jobs outside the home and pay taxes to the Social Security fund are entitled to their own benefits, but some have found it more advantageous to take half of their husband's entitlement. Because many women earn lower salaries and interrupt their careers during child-rearing years, their Social Security payments often don't average out to even half what they would receive as a dependent.

Women's organizations are battling this situation saying that it is unfair. They don't think women should be penalized for time off from work for essential family duties. "Motherhood and apple pie may be sacred in America," a critic told Congress, "but neither provide security in later life."

Tish Sommers, coordinator of a task force on older women for the National Organization of Women, notes that all wage earners—whether male or female—pay into Social Security at the same rate. "But," she says, "when more than one person works in the family, retirement income may be no greater than if only the presumed breadwinner paid into the system. The employed wife receives no benefit for her contribution."

There are an estimated one million cases in America where an elderly wife who worked can receive more from Social Security as a dependent than she can by claiming her own benefit. Here is a typical case: A retired man whose salary averaged $9,000 a year during his working years receives $531.80 a month. This represents his benefit plus an additional 50 percent for his dependent wife. In another case, both the husband and wife were employed. He earned $6,000 and she earned $3,000. Their monthly benefits, computed individually, would total only $444.50.

"The elderly wife gets nothing extra for her taxes," Miss Sommers complains. "We pay twice and collect once. The inequity is a real one."

Some critics claim that the Social Security system operates under antiquated laws dating from a time when women did not work much outside the home. Over the years, revisions have not kept pace with the changes in our society.

Now, 43 percent of American women between sixteen and sixty-four years of age are employed, and 38 percent of the work force is female, according to the U.S. Department of Labor. Figures from the Census Bureau show that nine out of ten women will hold a job at some time in their lives.

Women are also much more likely to be supporting families now than in the past. The divorce rate has more than doubled since 1965, and a fourth of the divorces occur after more than fifteen years of marriage. With the trend toward no-fault divorce, a woman may receive little or no alimony. And, after spending her married years taking care of a home and family, she may find herself entering the job market with few marketable skills.

47

The Census now shows that about 7.2 million U.S. families—one in every eight—are now headed by a woman. That represents a 46 percent increase over just ten years ago. Since women live longer, on the average, than men, they are more likely to be alone as they grow older. Only 66.5 percent of women aged fifty-five to sixty-four are still living with their husbands.

A widow who has been drawing half of her husband's Social Security benefit loses that after he dies. She will receive only his entitlement, even though her expenses may decrease only slightly. (A 1975 Supreme Court ruling now requires the Social Security system to pay survivors benefits to a widower with children who has been dependent on his wife for support.)

Various women's organizations have been attempting to persuade Congress to recognize the special problems retired women have with Social Security. They have pointed out that the success of the system can be measured only by how well it serves the majority of our citizens. And in the United States, women comprise 59 percent of the population over sixty-five and nearly two-thirds of those over seventy-five. The Census notes that of the five million elderly who live in poverty, more than two-thirds are women, mostly widows.

Women who are suddenly on their own in later years, because of divorce or the death of their husbands, have a particularly difficult time under the current Social Security regulations. Widows receive survivor's benefits, but divorcees often don't. If you are divorced and your ex-husband dies, you can collect survivor's benefits at age sixty only if you were married at least twenty years.

Chapter 5

No More Lost Pensions

The growth of private pension funds in the U.S. has been spectacular. In 1950, pension plans covered 9.8 million workers, or 22 percent of the work force. By 1974, the number of workers participating in pension plans had grown to more than 30 million, or about half of the nation's employed.

Proportionately, pension fund assets grew from $12.1 billion in 1950 to $130 billion in 1974, and are expected to reach more than $200 billion by 1980. They have become a major factor in the economy of this country, and in the minds of workers who are counting on them in their retirement years.

But the spectacular growth has been accompanied by spectacular problems. The Senate Committee on Labor and Public Work investigating private pension funds in 1974 revealed a shocking fact: millions of American workers who were counting on pensions offered by their employers were not receiving a penny when they retired. The pension plans weren't regulated by the government, and workers—some of whom had worked at companies for as long as 30 years—were frequently dismissed just before they were eligible to collect their hard-earned pensions.

The committee also reported that fewer than half of the workers in the U.S. are covered by pension plans of any kind. A full 54 percent of all single retirees and 44 percent of all retired couples were living on Social Security payments only.

The Labor and Public Works Committee took special note of this at a hearing in 1974. It reported: "Private pension income may mean the difference between a retirement which can provide a comfortable standard of living or one that is barely adequate. Yet many workers in private industry are not covered by pension plans and many of those who are participating in such plans will never receive any retirement benefits."

These findings led to passage of the Employe Retirement Income Security Act of 1974 (ERISA), sponsored by senators Jacob Javits of New York and Harrison A. Williams of New Jersey. Dubbed the "Employees' Bill of Rights," it is designed to prevent employes from being cheated out of their pensions and eventually will regulate the management of pension funds.

The ERISA covers more than 300,000 existing private pension plans and any that will be created in the future. It establishes concrete standards for participation in a pension and rules on vesting, or the length of service required before an employee is fully entitled to the money in his pension account. Before the ERISA came into being, many companies set their own vesting standards and were able to change them on a whim. Even more highly respectable companies were found to be engaged in pension-plan tactics that Congress found unethical. The Labor Department uncovered hundreds of cases where employees were being fired only weeks before retirement, losing their pension rights.

One woman told the committee that she had worked for a department store twenty-seven years when it suddenly decided to close. Although she had fulfilled the pension service requirement of twenty-five years, she was a year and ten months short of age sixty-five. Instead of receiving a pension, she had to settle for a small severance check.

"There was nothing she could do," said Rep. William J. Randall, chairman of the House Select Committee on Aging, at a later hearing. "She was left out in the cold."

In another instance that came to light during the investigation, a communications firm was found to be sadly remiss in living up to its pension promises. This company offered full vesting in the pension fund after fifteen years of service and age forty. But of 152,028 who had participated in the plan from the beginning, 108,035 left the company without any benefits. Of that group, 2,284 had more than fifteen years with the company and should have been fully vested. Another 4,592 had at least ten years of service, and 18,778 had been with the company for more than five years.

White-collar, non-union workers were found to be most likely to lose their pensions by being forced to retire early or released during cutbacks. Union members fared better, but they, too, were sometimes vulnerable. Only a third of the American work force employed in 1972 had guaranteed vesting rights by retirement age, according to a study made by the Census Bureau. Among workers who were at least fifty years old and facing retirement in a few years, only half had vested rights.

The Employee Retirement Income Security Act protects your benefits if the pension plan should go bankrupt. Pension payments up to $750 a month are guaranteed by the U.S. government if anything should happen to prevent the fund from sending your check.

The law doesn't require a company to start a pension plan but, if it already has one, it must make good on its promises. A pension is no longer considered a privilege granted at the employer's whim, but rather an employee's right.

All employees covered by a pension plan are guaranteed a portion of it after just one year's service after age twenty-five, with gradual increases until they are fully vested in fifteen years. There are some exceptions to this rule, so you should check with your company to see how you are affected.

If an employee wants to change jobs but hasn't done so because he feared losing his pension rights, he need fear no longer. Under ERISA, the company must inform the Social Security Administration of any pension rights he has accumulated. This applies no matter how many jobs an employee may hold before retiring. However, you might not be able to collect these pensions until you apply for Social Security benefits. This is still at the company's discretion.

The ERISA also states that anyone who believes he has

been cheated out of pension rights can take the company to court. If the employee wins the case, the company will probably have to pay any legal fees that the challenger incurred during litigation. Employees in a pension fund also have the right to have the pension's status explained to them at any time, in simple, straightforward language.

WOMEN AND PENSIONS

Women have special pension problems, whether they are surviving wives of a pensioner or they have earned a pension in their own right.

First there are loopholes in the pension law that can cause widows to lose survivors' benefits even though a husband has specifically asked that she be included.

In a hearing before the House Select Committee on Aging in October 1975, Paul S. Nathanson, executive director of the National Senior Citizens Law Center, gave a specific example of how this occurred. He told of a man who had worked for the same company thirty years and who was fully vested in his pension plan. At retirement, he joined a survivor option because he wanted to make certain his wife would be covered if he died. He lived only a year and a half after retirement. But when his widow asked that the pension check be sent to her, she was told that the option was applicable only if the pensioner lives for at least two years after retirement.

Arlene T. Shadoan, staff attorney for the National Senior Citizens Law Center, thinks drastic revisions need to be made in women's pensions. Ms. Shadoan testified before a House Committee: "Private pension plans in general are not satisfactory sources of retirement income for women, primarily because the private pension plans are associated with higher-paying jobs, and full-time, continuous service in the work force. Few women are in the higher-paying jobs covered by these plans."

Even those who are have problems. They often receive lower payments from a pension when they retire or they must contribute more to the fund while working. This is because pensions are figured on an actuarial basis, and women live longer than men. Both these practices have been ruled in violation of Title VII of the Civil Rights Act by both the Equal Opportunity Commission and by a federal district court in California.

Even so, the Labor Department has said that the practices do not violate the sex-discrimination provisions of the Equal Pay Act of 1963. The department has said that companies have every right to treat women differently in pension matters because of their longer life span. Ms. Shadoan suggests that, if women feel they are being treated unjustly by their company's pension rules, they should take it to court.

IRA—YOUR OWN PENSION PLAN

The 30 million Americans who work for companies that offer pension plans now have immediate financial protection, thanks to ERISA. But what about the remaining 30 million who work for firms that don't provide pensions?

These workers are now able to start a pension fund of their own, called an Individual Retirement Account, or IRA. The law allows them to place 15 percent of their annual income up to $1,500 into a retirement fund. This money immediately begins earning interest, but federal income taxes on it are deferred until the employee retires and begins collecting monthly payments. An IRA account can't be touched until an employee is 59½ years old, or it will be subject to stiff tax penalties. The money must be withdrawn when the worker reaches age seventy at the latest.

"By assuring the average worker that he will get more than one pension at his retirement—one from Social Security and one or more from private retirement programs—we will have taken a major step forward in securing the goal of adequate income to the aged," Sen. Javits noted.

Dozens of IRA plans are available, and anyone planning to set one up should be very careful about what he's getting into.

Some IRA plans are deferred annuities similar to those

offered by insurance companies. Most companies offer *ten-year* annuities that guarantee set monthly payments for ten years to the annuitant or his survivor. There are also *joint life* and *survivorship* annuities that guarantee income while either the husband or wife is alive. But this kind of annuity is often arranged so that a survivor receives only a portion, usually half or two-thirds—of what was paid to the couple, because the wife is expected to live longer.

You can set up an IRA at a bank, which will then pay you interest on the money you've deposited in the account.

An IRA can also be established through a mutual fund, but your money is subject to the same risks as any other funds you might invest. And, you usually will have to pay the stockbroker a commission.

Once a person with an IRA retires, he can elect to take the money in a lump sum or have it paid to him in monthly installments. If he takes the entire amount, it will be subject to capital-gains taxes and income taxes, which can be spread out over five years, or he can put it into an annuity if he likes.

Under IRA rules, if an employee has worked for a company with a pension plan and has vested rights, he can quit and transfer his pension funds into his own IRA. Then he can begin a second IRA so long as his new employer is not contributing to his pension fund.

The ERISA allows companies without pension plans to establish IRAs for any number of workers. They can pay all of the money into the IRA for them or a portion of it. The payments needn't be the same to each employee.

If neither husband nor wife works for a company offering a pension plan, both are eligible for IRAs. They can put a maximum of $1,500 a year each into separate IRAs, giving them $3,000 a year tax-free to start a retirement fund.

KEOGH PLAN

The Keogh Plan or HR 10, is similar to IRA, but it is for self-employed businessmen and professionals and those who run their own businesses in their spare time. This might include, for example, doctors, dentists, plumbers, or a full-time bank employee who writes books or advertising copy on his own time.

As with IRA, you are allowed to deposit 15 percent of your salary into the Keogh retirement plan. However, the big difference is the amount you can contribute tax-free: 15 percent of your annual income up to $7,500, instead of $1,500.

Even if you earn very little in a spare-time business, you can benefit from the Keogh Plan. That's because the 15 percent requirement is waived up to $750. Thus, if you only earn $750 a year, the entire amount can be placed in the fund and you won't have to pay taxes on it until you retire.

All Keogh plans must be set up as retirement funds with some kind of financial institution. As with the IRA, this may be an insurance company, mutual fund, bank or savings and loan association. You can't withdraw your money before the age of 59½ without paying stiff tax penalties. An owner-employee of a business—someone who owns at least 10 percent of the company—must begin taking money out of the Keogh Plan at age 70½ even if he continues to work. An employee, one who owns less than 10 percent, can keep his money in the fund until he retires, even if he is older than age 70½.

The Keogh Plan also permits you to put in extra "voluntary" contributions up to $250 a year. These voluntary payments are taxable, but the interest they earn won't be taxed until the money is withdrawn.

You can withdraw these voluntary payments at any time without tax penalties, but the interest the money earns must remain in the retirement account.

A person who employs a relative in his business can establish a Keogh retirement account for that relative. This is something that can be of great advantage to a husband-wife team who both work for their business. Each could establish a Keogh account and place a total of up to $15,000 a year, tax-free, into a retirement fund.

Like the IRA, you can't begin withdrawing money from a Keogh fund until you reach 59½ without paying a tax penalty.

The Internal Revenue Service has established tables to

calculate how much you can withdraw from a Keogh fund in monthly payments. There's no need to establish an annuity unless you want to. Once you begin receiving monthly payments, you must pay income tax on what you receive based on the laws that govern annuities. These regulations are complex, but the general rule is that you pay tax only on the amount that was not taxed previously as income.

If, for example, you have an $80,000 account and want to receive $8,000 a year for 10 years, you won't have to pay income tax on the portion of it that is voluntary contributions. You have *already* paid taxes on the voluntary contributions. The Keogh Plan allows you to receive tax-free payments for three full years if you have paid enough voluntary funds into the account to equal that many payments.

A person can also elect to take the retirement fund in a lump sum. With the exception of the voluntary portion, this money is taxed as income. But you can spread it out as income over ten years.

A Keogh Plan isn't the answer for everyone, particularly for professionals or businessmen with high incomes, who might prefer the tax advantages of incorporation. But for a moonlighter, a Keogh Plan is an excellent way to start a tax-free retirement account.

Chapter 6

The War Against Ageism (Some Legislative Victories)

"Ageism is as odious as racism and sexism," says feisty Rep. Claude Pepper of Florida. To do something about "ageism," the seventy-seven-year-old Congressman pushed through the House of Representatives a bill to end the long-established policy of most U.S. industry to compel employees to retire at age sixty-five.

He had been advocating such legislation for many years, but only in 1977, with groups like the Gray Panthers beginning to flex their political muscle, did his bill get out of committee—and then it sailed through the House with barely a nay. The 22.5 million Americans over sixty-five, more than 10 percent of the population, were beginning to make their presence known.

Two days later, the Senate passed a similar bill, amending the Age Discrimination in Employment Act of 1967. President Carter then signed the bill, which prohibits mandatory retirement in the private sector before age seventy. For most federal employees, forced retirement is prohibited at any age. The new law is effective Jan. 1, 1979, in most cases. Exempted from the provisions are tenured college teachers (who will be covered after July 1, 1982) and executives who are entitled to an immediate, irrevocable pension or other benefit of $27,000 or more a year, excluding Social Security.

The new legislation, of course, has a potential impact mainly on the 4.1 million employees in the U.S. between the

57

ages of sixty and sixty-four, because they can't be compelled to retire at sixty-five. Moreover, some of the nation's eight million retirees over the age of sixty now may choose to reenter the labor force.

Although the Labor Department was estimating that only about 200,000 people between sixty-five and seventy will actually keep working as a result of the new law, other estimates were higher. Many businessmen and unionists feared the consequences. Businessmen worried about such things as potential roadblocks to advancement of younger workers and middle managers. Unions worried that the higher mandatory-retirement age would encroach on negotiated labor contracts.

The higher cutoff for mandatory retirement could be offset to a large extent by new employer inducements for workers to retire. Economic factors have always been a major consideration in workers' decisions to retire or to continue working. Those who could afford to retire before age sixty-five, with substantial pension benefits, had been doing so in increasing numbers in recent years.

At General Motors, with its negotiated early-retirement plan, the average retirement age is below sixty. Early retirement is also common among governmental workers when the benefits are attractive. The new ban on mandatory retirement at age sixty-five notwithstanding, the only development likely to reverse the trend toward voluntary early retirement would be economic hardship. A prolonged inflationary spiral, for example, could cause a substantial number of potential retirees to worry about the future purchasing power of their retirement income—and consequently cause them to remain on the job longer than they planned.

Managements that faced having workers over age sixty-five for the first time became worried about the costs this could add to employee-benefit plans. Although the new law doesn't resolve the complex issues of retirement-plan coverage for those over sixty-five, the government has indicated that their continued participation in retirement-benefit accrual probably isn't required—except perhaps in supplemental plans where employers match the contributions of employees.

Generally, the payment of retirement benefits will merely be deferred, with no adverse impact on the employer's costs. But eventually, older workers' pressure and further legislation may require employers to revise their retirement plans to give credit for service after age sixty-five.

Hospitalization and disability benefits are a more irksome matter for employers, as coverage of employees over sixty-five could add significantly to costs. Conversely, the employee could have considerably better coverages than retired persons covered only by Medicare. For one thing, many company health plans, unlike Medicare, cover dental expenses.

But for hospital and medical costs, many company plans already provide that coverage for those over age sixty-five is limited to filling certain gaps in Medicare coverage. Costs wouldn't change for these companies unless they expanded the coverage.

Disability plans that discontinue coverage at age sixty-five will probably have to be revised, and this could add substantially to corporate costs. With the higher age limit for compulsory retirement, moreover, disabled employees would be eligible to receive benefits for a longer period of time. Life-insurance coverage also could become more costly for employers as the work force becomes older. But a phasing-out of benefits at sixty-five or thereabout is likely to continue because of the high cost of full coverage for older employees.

The implications of a higher mandatory-retirement floor are clearly a mixed bag for employers. The same might be said for the effects on the economy in general, for certain benefits could offset the potential impact on unemployment, for example.

"Here you have a certain segment of your population that suffers a very precipitous decline in income when they retire at sixty-five," says Fabian Linden, director of consumer research at the Conference Board, a business-research organization. "If you extend their work lives by three years, you are

59

increasing the total consumption level of the entire economy and of these people in particular."

The result could be added impetus to the growing economic power of the over-sixty generation, Mr. Linden says, and these people will be apt to spend more, stimulating the economy. "If you reduce the gap between retirement and mortality," he says, "it's less necessary to save because you are less concerned that you are going to be impoverished by inflation."

Although the raising of the mandatory-retirement age could worsen unemployment in the short run, some economists believe the long-term effect will be favorable. For one thing, the lower birthrate of the 1960s will almost certainly produce a decline in the number of young people entering the work force. The number of teen-agers in 1987 will be 24.2 million, down from 29.3 million in 1977. Moreover, the number of persons between fifty and sixty-five will decline slightly. This suggests that the workers over sixty-five could pick up the slack in the lower age group, which tends to produce both senior management and the most skilled workers.

Late in 1977, the Conference Board issued results of a survey of 5,000 households showing that a sizable majority of Americans oppose a mandatory retirement age. Surprisingly, the strongest opposition came from the young.

The survey asked the question: "At what age do you think people should be retired?"

The 1978 legislation outlawing compulsory retirement at age sixty-five was just the latest in a series of steps. The 1967 Age Discrimination in Employment Act prohibited job discrimination against workers in the forty-to-sixty-five range.

"The young people of this country are so willing to shove the elderly off into a rest home," says Rep. Edward P. Beard of Rhode Island, a member of the House Select Committee on Aging. "Priorities and attitudes of the younger people in this country need to change. We all need to work for the best interest of all of the elderly Americans."

The government, spurred by a very determined group of

Distribution of Responses

	At Age:			No Fixed Age
	60	**65**	**70**	
Total Respondents	**15.4%**	**16.7%**	**4.3%**	**63.6%**
Age of Household Head				
Under 25	12.9	8.0	4.0	75.1
25-34	14.1	10.3	4.3	71.3
35-44	17.0	16.1	2.7	64.2
45-54	18.8	16.2	3.4	61.6
55-64	17.5	22.1	4.2	56.2
65 and over	8.2	31.5	9.2	51.1
Household Income				
Under $5,000	21.0	18.9	3.9	56.2
$5,000-$10,000	16.7	19.5	5.1	58.7
10,000-15,000	15.6	15.8	4.8	63.8
15,000-20,000	14.6	16.2	3.4	65.8
20,000-25,000	14.4	13.1	4.4	68.1
25,000 and Over	11.4	16.6	3.7	68.3
Occupation of Household Head				
White Collar	11.6	14.4	4.8	69.2
Blue Collar	21.3	14.0	2.5	62.2

retirees, has taken steps to change those attitudes. Committees on aging in both houses of Congress regularly hold hearings around the country to gather information on senior citizens' problems. Two White House Conferences on Aging have been held in recent years, both of which clarified the needs of the elderly and recommended remedial action.

In 1965, Congress enacted the Older Americans Act to establish goals for aiding the elderly and to create an office to administer various programs. The new Administration on Aging was given responsibility for meeting ten objectives:

1. To provide an adequate income in retirement so that Americans won't have to live a substandard existence in their later years.

2. Make the best possible physical and mental-health treatment facilities available without regard to the patient's economic status.

3. Provide suitable housing, located in areas that are convenient to shopping, at a price the elderly can afford.

4. Provide proper institutional care for all who need it, regardless of ability to pay.

5. Offer employment opportunities without age discrimination in hiring or wages.

6. Guarantee health, honor and dignity in retirement after a person has spent a lifetime contributing to the economy of the country.

7. Assist retired people in pursuing meaningful civic, cultural and recreational activities.

8. Establish efficient community services for the aged, especially low-cost, convenient mass transportation.

9. Give the elderly access to the latest research findings that can sustain and improve their health and well-being.

10. Guarantee retirees freedom, independence, and the free exercise of individual initiative in planning and managing their lives.

These are lofty goals and, though the government has a long way to go, some positive steps have been taken to meet the special needs of the elderly since the Social Security Act was passed in 1935. Here is a status report on what the government is doing:

TAXES—The Senate Select Committee on Aging reported in 1975 that "perhaps one-half of all elderly individuals pay more taxes than legally required." This happens, the committee said, because many elderly taxpayers are "unaware of legitimate deductions, credits, and exemptions that can save them precious dollars."

Little-known tax deductions that may be of special interest to older people include:

—Physician-prescribed modifications on a home, as long as they don't increase the value of the home. This might include a special elevator, humidifier or special air filter. Be sure to get—and keep—written proof that these were prescribed by a doctor.

—Medical-insurance premiums, including the amount you may have paid for Part B of Medicare. You may deduct half of these premium costs up to $150.

—Hearing aids, batteries and their maintenance.

—Transportation costs to and from doctors, dentists, laboratories and pharmacies. (Note: None of these medical deductions can be taken unless your total medical expenses exceed 3% of your adjusted gross income.)

—Transportation costs to a volunteer job. You can deduct either the exact amount you paid for public transportation, or seven cents a mile, plus parking expenses, if you used your automobile.

—People over sixty-five receive an additional $750 personal exemption whether or not they itemize deductions.

—Those over sixty-five also qualify for a Retirement Income Tax Credit of 15% on certain types of income, such as pensions, interest, rents, annuities and dividends. Consult the Internal Revenue Service publication Number 524, "Retirement Income Credit" for full details.

—If you sell your home after turning sixty-five you may be eligible for a tax break. You don't have to pay any capital-gains taxes if you receive up to $35,000 more from the sale than you originally paid. Thus, if you paid $20,000 for a house in 1960 and sell it for $55,000 at age sixty-five, you make a

$35,000 profit that is tax-free. This exemption only applies if you have used the home as your principal residence for five of the eight years preceding the sale.

You can get additional information on all tax matters by calling the toll-free number listed in your telephone directory under the U.S. Internal Revenue Service. Representatives are available at all local IRS offices to assist you in preparing your tax forms. Detailed information on tax benefits for the elderly can be found in pamphlet Number 554, "Protecting Older Americans Against Overpayment of Income Taxes," available for sixty cents by writing to the Superintendent of Documents, U.S. Government Printing Office, Washington, D.C. 20042.

MEDICARE—Medicare, part of the Social Security System, helps Americans over sixty-five and severely disabled people under sixty-five, to pay for the high cost of health care.

The hospital-insurance portion of the Medicare program helps pay for the care you receive as a patient in a hospital and for specific follow-up treatment after you are released.

The medical insurance portion of the program helps pay physician's fees, outpatient hospital services and many other medical items not covered under hospital insurance.

Everyone who is sixty-five or older and entitled to Social Security or railroad retirement benefits gets hospital insurance automatically without paying monthly premiums. You needn't be retired to qualify.

People who are sixty-five and older but who aren't automatically entitled to the hospital insurance can buy the protection for a small monthly sum. To do so, they must enroll in the medical-insurance program.

Others who can receive Medicare protection include:

—People under sixty-five if they have received disability benefits for at least twenty-four consecutive months.

—Kidney patients who need dialysis or kidney transplants.

Additional information on Medicare benefits and eligibility can be obtained from your local Social Security office.

Though it goes a long way toward providing the elderly and disabled with comprehensive health care, Medicare isn't a panacea, as Sen. Edmund Muskie of Maine told the Senate Select Committee on Aging. "Medicare and Medicaid, like the rest of our health-care system, suffer from inadequacies, contradictions and a strong bias in favor of institutional care," Muskie said.

Muskie noted that benefits have steadily decreased as medical costs have risen in recent years. In 1969, he said, Medicare covered 46.2 percent of the total health costs of older people. But by 1975, he noted, the coverage had decreased to only 38.1 percent.

NATIONAL NUTRITIONAL PROGRAM—Scattered around the country are various organizations that provide low-cost, nutritional meals to older people who can't afford well-balanced meals. These nutritional projects are part of a $187.5 million federal program to help make certain that retirees are adequately nourished. There are more than 665 projects funded by various states under this federal program, providing an average of 245,000 hot meals a day to older Americans. Sixty-four percent of those meals were served to elderly Americans living below the federal poverty standard.

These meals, usually served in senior-citizen centers and school cafeterias, are available to people over the age of sixty and are administered by state agencies on the aging. Most programs provide transportation to and from the food center for elderly participants.

Usually the meals cost less than they would if they were fixed at home. In 1976, they were averaging just over $1.00 per meal in most parts of the country. No one is turned away because they can't afford the price of the meal.

Not only does this program provide recipients with a balanced diet, but also the group meals give them an opportunity for companionship. Many participants say they look forward as much to the sociability as to the hot meal.

Thomas J. Farley, director of Milwaukee's Food Services Division, is the head of one of the most successful nutrition programs in the nation. A good lunch for that city's senior citizens is no farther than the nearest neighborhood school. More than 150 of the city's 170 schools open their doors to senior citizens for lunch. And this project isn't funded by the state or federal government; it is self-supporting. The elderly pay the same price for their meals as the teachers do—fifty cents for the food and ten cents for a beverage.

"The over-sixty crowd are the people who built our schools with their taxes," Farley says, noting that the city decided to give them a return on their tax dollars. More than 3,000 senior citizens take a short walk each weekday to get a hot meal. One older man, who hardly ever left the house before he joined the lunch program, says he is feeling better physically because he gets exercise on his daily walk to school.

Participants in the Milwaukee lunch program believe that it helps overcome the isolation that many retirees feel, and it lets students become better acquainted with the elderly.

"We find that the elderly are a delightful addition to our lunch program," Farley says. "Everything seems to please them, and they are responsive to the kids."

The elderly concur. "I don't know if we could take the kids all day long," one says, "but it sure is wonderful to hear youthful exuberance for a change."

The federal nutrition program is designed for lower-income retirees, but self-supporting senior-citizen centers around the country have also begun to offer low-cost meals. Your state agency on aging can give you information concerning such programs.

SUBSIDIZED HOUSING—The Housing and Community Development Act of 1974 made far-reaching changes in the housing situation for the elderly.

Under provisions of the act, the Department of Housing and Urban Development provides housing subsidies for low-income elderly people. Depending on the income of the recipient, the government rent subsidy can be as much as 80 percent of the cost per month.

HUD was also authorized in 1974 to make construction loans of up to $800 million to build low-rental housing units for elderly people with low incomes. In fiscal 1976, Congress appropriated $360 million to help finance construction of housing for the elderly that is convenient to shopping and transportation.

Those who are eligible pay no more than 25 percent of their income for rent, including utilities. Local housing authorities maintain lists of available units and can provide information as to how you can qualify.

NATIONAL INSTITUTE ON AGING—In 1974, Congress created the National Institute on Aging to function as a branch of the National Institute of Health, the agency that sponsors nearly half the health and medical research in this country. The Institute on Aging is separately funded and is responsible for conducting and supporting biomedical, social and behavioral research and training relating to the aging process.

Specifically, government researchers are studying how to control and prevent degenerative diseases of old age such as arteriosclerosis, high blood pressure, cancer, cataracts and senility.

The government spends several million dollars each year for this investigation of the diseases of aging. Medical researchers are attempting to discover why cells deteriorate, why the arteries harden and why certain metabolic changes occur as we grow older.

The prospects are hopeful. Dr. Gairdner B. Moment, of Goucher College's department of biological sciences has written: "The goal of making it possible to age well will be achieved, so that a satisfying old age, both physically and mentally, will be the good fortune of people everywhere."

67

Chapter 7

Beating the Retirement Blues

"The problem is that one day you're in the harness, pulling your own weight, and then you find yourself put out to pasture with nothing that you have to do. You don't feel that you're worth a damn."

So said a Californian after his forced retirement, expressing the pangs felt by many a retiree in a culture that stresses the value of work and personal contribution.

"Work binds the individual more closely to reality [and] the human community," Sigmund Freud wrote in "Civilization and Its Discontents" in 1929.

More recently, the phenomenon has been noted by the American Medical Association. In backing a federal lawyer's lawsuit to keep his job beyond age seventy, the AMA said, "Considerable medical evidence is available to indicate that the sudden cessation of productive work and earning power of an individual, caused by compulsory retirement at the chronological age of sixty-five, often leads to physical and emotional deterioration and premature death."

DEATH OF A MANAGER

Helena Sexauer says her husband began dying the day his boss told him he should retire early from his job as operations manager in the accounting department of an auto maker in Michigan. Wilbur Sexauer was fifty-nine.

During the six months before his retirement, Mrs. Sexauer said in an account in *The National Observer*, her husband didn't sleep or eat properly.

"He couldn't finish a sandwich at one sitting, and he complained that his stomach felt like it was falling," she said. In the final five weeks of anguish before he was to retire in early 1973, she added, he lost thirty pounds.

"He told me he was going in and sign the papers the Tuesday after Memorial Day weekend," Mrs. Sexauer said. "But for Bill, Tuesday never came." Sexauer's body was found in the closed garage of his home, with the car engine running.

"The job was as much a part of my husband as his home. He loved both and lived for each."

The couple had planned for a later retirement. "We were going to keep our home, of course, and we'd put a down payment on a condominium in Florida," Mrs. Sexauer said. "We thought we'd live quietly, alternating between the two. We could have made it, too, but when they forced the early retirement on him, well, it was impossible. The funds simply weren't there."

Sexauer's annual income had been around $40,000, she says, but the forced retirement, which came after a new boss was named in Sexauer's department, would have cut the income to about $14,000 a year.

Her husband's suicide left Mrs. Sexauer bewildered, and she later sued his employer to protest the forced retirement. She ultimately dropped the suit after the Internal Revenue Service said it would reassess her husband's estate based on revenue that might come in a settlement.

Mrs. Sexauer has since formed an organization called FEAR, an acronym for Fair Executive Action for Retirement. "The more people I meet—and I have met many, many since stories about the suit appeared in the press—the more I realize that executives and their wives live in constant fear of that early retirement."

Mrs. Sexauer says corporations should begin training their executives at age thirty-five to prepare for retirement and even go so far as to help them enter another field if necessary at age fifty-five.

The Sexauer case may have been extreme, and it certainly received more attention than most retirements. But a study at the University of California at Berkeley found that many retirees actually mourn the loss of employment as if they are grieving over the death of a loved one. The study found that many retirees feel as though part of them has died. The retirees in the study referred to themselves in the past tense, saying "I was" or "I used to be."

FEAR OF AGING

This isn't so surprising in a youth-centered society that emphasizes vitality, good looks and rapid change. Many Americans suffer from what R.O. Bechman, who is affiliated with the Senior Service Foundation in Miami, Fla., calls gerontophobia, or the fear of growing old.

Indeed, a State University of New York survey found that 40 percent of Americans dread growing old. So intense is this fear in many younger people in the U.S., Mr. Bechman says, that they shun or ignore the aged. This phobic reaction toward aging is reflected also in the media and on Madison Avenue, where older people are often portrayed as toothless, constipated, half-daft individuals who contribute nothing worthwhile.

Some other societies deal more effectively with their aged. The Hindus look forward to the day when they can retire from workaday life and concentrate on spiritual development. And most Oriental and African societies elevate the elderly to revered social, political and economic roles.

Anthropologist Margaret Mead, who is in her mid-seventies, suggests that one reason women have a longer life expectancy than men is that they can continue to do something they are used to doing, regardless of age, whereas men are abruptly cut off from their accustomed pursuits.

Because work—and the prestige and money that go with it—are so very important in American society, many professionals studying the problems of the elderly have concluded that mandatory retirement is an archaic practice, especially in an era when people are living longer and are able to fully contribute well beyond the age of sixty-five.

"Many of our seventy-year-olds today are more like their fifty-year-old counterparts at the beginning of the century, due to improved nutrition, health care and environmental sanitation," says a specialist on aging at Syracuse University. "Whistler's mother, who epitomizes old age, was only forty-four when she sat for the painting." As an alternative, many experts suggest that older people be eased into retirement gradually.

Dr. Raymond Wing, an Easton, Pa., psychiatrist, told a White House Conference on Aging that "mandatory retirement serves as a shock and gives a feeling of inferiority not only to the retiree, but to his spouse and family as well." By contrast, he says, "retirement for disability or from choice does not seem to result in the psychological state that produces the feeling of second-class citizenship."

GRADUAL RETIREMENT

Alfred H. Foxcroft, president of Leisure World Stars Inc., a Laguna Hills, Calif., company that provides leisure programs for the elderly, suggests a voluntary arrangement that would gradually decrease the number of hours worked as a person grows older. From age fifty-five to sixty, for example, an employe would work only thirty-five hours a week, receiving 87.5 percent of the salary he received when he worked a forty-hour week. Every five years, Mr. Foxcroft suggests, his work week and salary could be readjusted downward. When the employe finally retired, he would have become accustomed to leisure time and a lower income.

Similarly, Dr. Wing says: "One wonders if a system whereby older persons are offered incentives to do useful work and penalties if they do not, would help put them back in the mainstream of life."

Alexander Reid Martin, a psychiatrist in Old Lyme,

Conn., believes that part of the difficulty in adjusting to retirement stems from an educational system that prepares us almost exclusively for life on the job. Our values, philosophies and attitudes toward social issues are all forged and tempered by education. The shorter workweek, early retirement and increasing longevity, he says, are combining to "establish a new world for which we are educationally unprepared." Educators have begun to realize this, and the federal government now sponsors programs at universities around the country to offer courses in preparing for retirement and old age.

No one wants to get old, or at least to suffer from the afflictions—both physical and psychological—that so often accompany old age. However, the trauma of suddenly being deprived of a useful purpose in life can be lessened by striving to develop healthy attitudes about yourself and your work.

There is evidence that American society's overweening veneration of work—for its own sake—is breaking down. Leisure time is more plentiful than in generations past, and most people are learning how to make better use of it and enjoy it. These people will have less difficulty adjusting to retirement.

A LESSENING WORK ETHIC?

Three professors at the University of Michigan who are experts in industrial and human relations recently published a study that found that reverence for the work ethic was on the decline. Professors W. Alan Randolf, Max S. Sortman Jr. and Barry Z. Posner noted that the work ethic stems from primitive times when work was necessary for survival. It "is on the verge of losing meaning and utility" in today's society, they wrote.

Instead of a work ethic, the professors said, we should develop a "worth ethic," emphasizing the importance of developing as human beings, not just workers.

"The worth ethic holds that people have worth by virtue of being human beings and not by virtue of some activity such as work, education, travel, or any other activity in which one might engage," they wrote. "It breaks down the traditional distinctions between time engaged in typical work activities and time engaged in nonwork activities. The worth ethic has as its rationale and purpose the creation and development of healthy and mature individuals, as opposed to the immature person who is passive, dependent, apathetic, destructive and rebellious."

The authors of the study suggest that long before retirement, people should begin to develop their unique skills and ideas, study things that interest them, interact with people on a nonworking basis, and find ways to contribute to society off the job.

Following this advice will not only enrich your working years and lay the groundwork for a happy retirement, it may enhance your physical health. Medical experts now believe that a great many diseases may be caused, or at least complicated by, too much stress. Meyer Friedman and Ray H. Rosenman, the heart specialists who wrote "Type A Behavior and Your Heart," say that an appreciation of yourself and of the world around you, in addition to your work, is of great importance in combating coronary artery disease. People who can't relax, who hustle busily around unable to enjoy their leisure time, were found to be much more prone to heart attacks and other diseases than their more easygoing contemporaries.

AN EASY TRANSITION

Dr. Barbara Armstrong, a specialist in family relationships at Akron (Ohio) University, believes that people who lead emotionally satisfying lives as young people will make a smooth transition to retirement. Those who haven't will have a harder time of it as they grow older. "Life satisfaction is a function of the individual personality," she says. "When you get older you don't change—you get like you always were, only more so."

Learning to enjoy life off the job will help you develop lifetime hobbies and interests that will stand you in good stead in retirement. One sociologist says that many retirees suffer psychological problems because they mistakenly think they can't—or shouldn't—do certain things because of their age.

Alden Whitman, former senior obituary writer for *The New York Times* and one who has had a chance to closely observe many elderly people, has written that those who adjusted well in retirement were people with a clear notion of who they were, what they were, why they were and where they were. He noted that they possessed a kind of inner strength that helped them to come to terms with themselves and the process of aging.

The Gray Panthers, headquartered in Washington, D.C., is trying to instill such inner resources in the elderly of America. Bee Wolfe, a 63-year-old social worker and Gray Panther member, says the group's goals are to end isolation, to create an awareness of political power, to help one another gain a sense of self-worth and to "realize that what's wrong is not in us, but in the society."

The Gray Panthers are trying to banish the notion that there's something shameful about growing old. "Bodies break down, we don't deny that," says member Lilliana Morrison, sixty-eight. "But I don't find that distasteful. Everybody's going to be young, middle-aged and old, and some people are going to be late-bloomers."

Max Friedson, a seventy-seven-year-old Miamian, is an active lobbyist for the elderly in the Florida legislature. He says he has learned from personal experience that one of the most debilitating and prevalent attitudes held by old people is a lack of self-esteem.

"The worst thing is feeling not wanted and not needed," he says. "Lonesomeness kills." The answer, as he sees it, is to stay busy and involved as long as you possibly can. Why rust when you can wear out?

Senator Hiram L. Fong of Hawaii told a White House Conference on Aging that retirees want to play a more active role in society. "More and more older Americans have greater capacity for involvement in life's affairs," he said. "Their children have left the nest, and the parents are free to follow new pursuits. Thanks to medical and scientific advances, people are living longer and are healthier. Their desire to enjoy life, to serve their fellow man, and to be a vital part of society's mainstream grows apace."

AGELESS CONTRIBUTIONS

To illustrate his point that the elderly needn't be relegated to a dependent, passive role, Sen. Fong noted that Sophocles didn't write "Oedipus Rex" until he was in his eighties, Chaucer wrote "Canterbury Tales" when he was sixty, Oliver Wendell Holmes Jr. was appointed to the U.S. Supreme Court when he was sixty-one and served until he was almost ninety, and Michelangelo was painting "The Last Judgement" after he had passed his eightieth birthday.

To that list we might add Benjamin Franklin, who invented bifocal lenses when he was seventy-eight, and such contemporaries as conductor Arthur Fiedler and comedian George Burns, who are in their eighties, and comedian Bob Hope, who is in his seventies.

Newly retired people often feel a general euphoria for the first two or three weeks after they are off the job. Then they suddenly are shocked to realize that they are in for a long, long retirement. Restlessness sets in. A trip seems like a good idea, but retirees who have made trips within the first month or two after retirement say it is better to wait six months or so before traveling. By then, a trip may be more essential because the restlessness may be more severe.

In North Port Charlotte, Fla., retirees who had become bored decided to change their circumstances. They wanted to set up an educational center where they could learn how to garden, sail, fish, do needlepoint and otherwise expand their interests and knowledge.

They approached the county for help, but were unable to get funding. So they decided to raise the money themselves. Just a year after a steering committee was formed, they had raised a million dollars. Now retirees by the hundreds take classes in dozens of courses, ranging from calculus to lawn care. The classes often are taught by retired experts, and the tuition is just enough to cover operating costs. It was so successful that the county commission finally made it part of the school system and helps support it financially.

REMOVING THE STIGMA

Retirees themselves and many government agencies are similarly attempting to remove the stigma of growing old in America. They want to remove the predominant image of retirees sitting in rocking chairs. The federal government has established Senior Centers around the country where retirees can meet for socializing or getting help with their problems. Many of these centers have formed volunteer organizations that help with civic projects. These centers are also storehouses of information on Social Security, Medicare, pensions, and employment matters. They frequently help provide meals under the federal nutrition program.

Most states have endorsed the concept that people should be prepared early for retirement and life away from a job and children. Some offer college courses in retirement preparation. The federal government has funded many of these programs at colleges and community colleges around the country. Many of these courses are tuition-free.

But the main thing that needs to be changed in America, sociologists say, is the attitude toward retirement, the attitude that only through work do we have value as human beings. The emphasis on work isn't unique in the U.S. (Germans are considered to have a similar propensity), and the attitude wasn't invented by the Puritans.

Arthur Toynbee, the historian, said that in the Middle Ages work became almost a religious obligation. Work is fine when it serves an end, he said, but it shouldn't be pursued for its own sake.

Americans have never been unanimous in their feelings about work, of course. A century ago, Henry David Thoreau preached the virtues of the quiet, leisurely life he led at Walden Pond. Thoreau suggested that the working man was no more than a machine driven to perform tasks automatically. Forget about what people think about you for not working, Thoreau advised, and his own attitude toward obsessive work prompted a famous Thoreau quotation:

"Public opinion is a weak tyrant compared with our own private opinion. The mass of men lead lives of quiet desperation." But Thoreau was something of a maverick in his time, and not too many people were listening, even in Concord, Mass.

More recently, Dr. Margaret Clark has conducted studies indicating a decline in such things as the morality associated with work. With the decline, she says, retirement should become less of a problem. Society will become oriented more toward leisure, and retired people will play a greater role in day-to-day living.

Meantime, most retirees find that keeping busy—with a new job, a hobby, volunteer work or whatever—is a key to being happy. Some even feel that "retirement" is a misnomer.

"Retirement means that you are withdrawing from life," one says. "That isn't true. We don't just fold up our tents and sneak off into the night."

A COLONEL'S NEW LIFE

Colonel Bill Royal, an Air Force retiree now in his seventies, continues to pursue his hobby of skin diving with a passion. Royal once decided to see if he could capture sharks in the open water and ride them like bucking broncos. Royal perfected that technique, then turned to something equally dangerous: cave diving.

Royal is one of the few men who have been able to dive to the bottom of Warm Mineral Springs in Florida, going to a depth of more than 230 feet. On one of his dives Royal discovered some ancient human remains. An amateur archaeologist, he knew that his findings might be significant. They were. Tests showed that Royal had discovered the oldest human fossils in America. Nowadays, Col. Royal is routinely called on to lead diving expeditions into the Springs and to lecture widely through the country.

Not everyone could, or should, lead such a vigorous life at seventy, but Col. Royal's experience illustrates the value of developing side interests early in life, as he did. It often isn't easy to develop new interests in later years.

Dr. Charles Taylor, a psychologist at Pennsylvania State University, has this advice: "The ideal way to deal with problems of retirement is to find reasonable substitutions for whatever satisfaction work and the world of work supplied. The end of one period (work) doesn't necessarily mark the beginning of another (retirement)."

STRAINS ON A MARRIAGE

Developing outside interests can also relieve strains that retirement can put on a marriage because of the changes wrought by the new style of living—and the aging process in general.

"I married him for better or worse, in sickness or health," goes a now-familiar refrain, "but for heavens sake, I didn't marry him for lunch!"

An unaccustomed full-time husband around the house, without long-cultivated interests to keep him occupied, can become quite a burden for the unsuspecting wife.

"He's looking over your shoulder all the time," says one wife in such a predicament. "He becomes an efficiency expert and tells you better ways to do it. He notices that you use too much bleach and soap when you do the laundry. He uses two phrases more often then any others, 'Where are you going?' and 'Where have you been?'

"It isn't quite the same as having your husband about the house on a weekend when he has a job. On Monday he returns to work. But when he retires, the quick excision from his work routine leaves him slightly dazed, and he really doesn't know what to do with all the time at his disposal."

Women, on the other hand, are prone to suffer from the "empty nest" syndrome after the children are grown. Many women find it a painful process to redirect their lives, which had been centered on the children. But this adjustment is usually made before the time the husband's retirement rolls around and grandchildren help to fill the void left by the absent children.

A secret to family adjustment in retirement is to share the household work but to stay out of each other's hair as much as possible. Vic Soloman of Long Island does a lot of work around the house, but he and his wife also spend time with separate recreational pursuits.

"I've had other interests in my life, but I started sailing when I was eight or nine in New Jersey, and it has been my major love," he says. "I bought my first sailboat in 1952—a twenty-footer. That's how I spend most of my time now."

These days, Soloman sails a catamaran. "I wanted one of the fastest sailboats around," he says. "A racing machine for two people. There are always things to do around a boat, so I don't have to worry about finding things to do."

Some retirees like the Solomans seem to escape the readjustment trauma. These are usually the people who have planned wisely. Says Soloman, "Most people don't plan ahead. They wait around and all of a sudden they're sixty-five. They have to retire and don't know what to do with themselves. You have to look ahead and know how to spend your time."

Chapter 8

Where to Live, What to Live In

Consider the scene at Century Village East, a haven in Florida for 9,000 retirees:

Abe Schawartz starts the afternoon off by leading a group of his fellow retirees in the R.S.V.P. kazoo band around the recreation room to the tune of "When the Saints Come Marching In." After kazoo practice, it's ceramics, painting or sewing. Then on to yoga class, a quick dip in the pool and a full evening of dancing with 1,000 or so participating.

At Century Village East, as profiled in a *Wall Street Journal* article, there's something for everyone every waking minute, from psychology class in the morning to a movie or stage show at night. The program includes more than 200 classes, lectures and special events a week. The clubhouse has a 1,600-seat theater, a 34-table billiards room, card rooms and classrooms. A recreation staff of 60 leads the activities.

Today, there are about 50 of these so-called full-living retirement communities, housing more than 500,000 retired Americans, mostly in the Sun Belt. The idea dates back to Sun City, Ariz., in the 1950s, but the trend really caught on in the 1970s.

Yet full-living communities aren't for everyone. The Roper poll found only 5 percent of Americans want to move to various types of retirement communities. The vast majority, 86 percent, want to live in an established community with a mixture of ages and types of people. Moreover, 60 percent of

81

Americans want to stay in the same area where they are now after retirement.

In any case, not everyone can afford a place like Century Village East. The average price for the one-bedroom or two-bedroom condominiums is $25,300, the monthly maintenance leases cost $38 and the recreation leases $33. There are also small charges for many classes and events.

But the charges are within the reach of many, and many Americans are obviously enjoying their retirement years at places like Century Village East, especially if they are in good enough health to participate in the activities.

Still, even if you have sufficient money and health to partake fully of the activities at a full-living community, you will be well advised to consider all alternatives carefully.

Dr. Jerry Jacobs, a sociologist at Syracuse University, conducted a study of such a community in the West, which he called "Fun City." He found that only about 10 percent of the 6,500 residents took part in any of the many planned activities at the community. Most spent their time at home, many of them bored or depressed.

"Down here, it doesn't make any difference when you eat or when you sleep," one resident said. "Because you aren't going any place. You aren't doing anything. And if I'm up all night reading and then sleep all day, what's the difference?"

Fun City illustrates a problem many people have at retirement communities of all kinds. The people feel cut off from the mainstream of life.

Moving away from the community where you were in the mainstream can be a problem in itself. Dr. Woodrow F. Hunter, a professor at the University of Michigan's Institute of Gerontology, says that many people who move away from a community where they have lived for years eventually change their minds and move back.

Fishing, golf or shuffleboard may be terrific avocations, but building a life around them may be a very different story. Roots are important to most people, and they can't easily be transplanted.

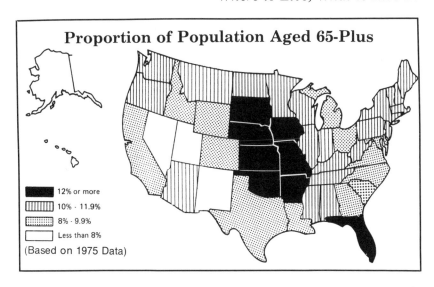

Proportion of Population Aged 65-Plus

- 12% or more
- 10% - 11.9%
- 8% - 9.9%
- Less than 8%

(Based on 1975 Data)

Dr. Hunter tells of a Detroit couple who decided to move to Florida on retirement to escape the cold weather and frenetic pace. They didn't move blindly. They checked out a community that had people from all around the country. They compared it with other parts of Florida and finally took a two-bedroom cottage at the community.

But within three months, they decided to move back to Detroit. Their children, grandchildren, friends and their past were all back there.

Retirement itself can be traumatic enough without the added disruption of leaving a longtime home community. Dr. Marvin Sussman, director of the Institute on the Family and the Bureaucratic Society at Case Western Reserve University, says people often regard retirement as a "demotion." They must adjust to a sharp reduction in income and an entirely new life role. This can lead to "withdrawal symptoms" as severe as those usually associated with a long-term illness, he says.

Cutting off your lifeline by moving to a new and unfamiliar location can make the situation worse, Dr. Sussman says. Whether you like to admit it or not, your energies are probably diminished, and the effort to seek out new friends may be considerable. You may like the idea of not seeing your children or grandchildren daily, but if they are hundreds of miles away, you may discover a big void in your life.

If you have lived in a community for some time, you have probably developed long-standing relationships with doctors, shopkeepers and service people, and it may take years to establish similar relationships in a new community. Cultivating new activities also can usually be easier in a community where you are known.

IF YOU DECIDE TO MOVE

Only one couple or person out of four moves to another city after retirement, according to Housing and Urban Development Department statistics, although seven out of ten families headed by someone over sixty-five own their own homes. Only one in ten of those retirees who move do it more than once.

If you are one of those who decides to move for one reason or another, you would do well to consider how the cost of living in your chosen area will compare with your present area. The following table gives some comparisons.

When you move—across town or across the country—you will be faced with many decisions, such as whether to take your furnishings along or buy new ones for your new home.

Edward N. Fleming, a retiree who has lived in both Arizona and Florida, says furniture turns over so rapidly in both states that it reminds him of a year-round fire sale. Fleming, who used to be an automobile salesman, decided he can make as much money buying and selling furniture as he did selling cars.

"Retired people," he says, "often move far from home, decide they don't like where they are, and sell their furniture because they can't afford to pay for moving it back. Or retired people find their furniture doesn't fit in the new home and have to sell it and buy new things."

Cost of Living For a Retired Couple in Selected Cities and Areas[1]
(Average cost in all U.S. cities = 100)

AREA	INDEX
Urban United States	100
Metropolitan areas	105
Nonmetropolitan areas[2]	86
Northeast:	
Boston, Mass	119
Buffalo, N.Y.	110
Hartford, Conn.	115
New York-N.E. New Jersey	118
Philadelphia, Pa.-New Jersey	107
Portland, Me.	104
Nonmetropolitan areas[2]	98
North Central:	
Cedar Rapids, Ia.	100
Chicago, Ill.-N.W. Indiana	101
Dayton, Ohio	96
Green Bay, Wis.	99
Minneapolis-St. Paul, Minn.	101
St. Louis, Mo.-Ill	100
Nonmetropolitan areas[2]	89
South:	
Atlanta, Ga.	91
Austin, Tex.	90
Baltimore, Md.	98
Baton Rouge, La.	88
Dallas, Tex.	94
Durham, N.C.	94
Houston, Tex.	93
Nashville, Tenn.	96
Orlando, Fla.	92
Washington, D.C.-Va.-Md.	103
Nonmetropolitan areas[2]	81
West:	
Bakersfield, Calif.	95
Denver, Colo.	97
Los Angeles-Long Beach, Calif.	103
San Diego, Calif.	99
San Francisco-Oakland, Calif.	110
Seattle-Everett, Wash.	104
Honolulu, Hawaii	113
Nonmetropolitan areas[2]	89

[1]Based on an intermediate budget for a retired couple (husband 65 or over), Autumn 1972. Preliminary estimates developed by U.S. Department of Labor, Bureau of Labor Statistics.

[2]Places with population of 2,500 to 50,000.

The furniture being sold often is antiques that are too cumbersome or otherwise inappropriate for the new home. Retirees end up losing money first by paying the initial shipping expenses and then by having to sell the furniture for less than it is worth.

If you consider relocating, it's a good idea to rent in the community of your choice for a year, say. This gives you an opportunity to sample the new way of life without permanently pulling up roots. You'll have an opportunity to thoroughly investigate an area—checking the cost of living, the availability of medical care and other services, the new climate—and to get to know your prospective neighbors.

You may even be able to rent your present home and apply that money toward the rent you are paying in the new community. If you decide to move back home after the trial period, you can do so without a major expense.

One New York couple thought they would like to move to Arizona, but they wanted to be certain before they took the big step. They decided to vacation in Arizona for a month to see what it was like.

They rented a hotel room and systematically began checking out the community. They went window-shopping in various areas in the community to see what the prices were and the kinds of things being sold. By looking at the newspapers every day, they learned of the community's social activity. The classified advertisements in the newspapers gave them an indication of the economic health of the community, and they were able to find out first hand about property taxes, inheritance taxes and the cost of living.

When they were satisfied that it was the kind of community they could be happy in, they rented for a year. The year convinced them that their first impression was correct, so they sold their house in New York and made Arizona their retirement home.

Some retirees who decide to stay in their home towns move from large homes into smaller houses or apartments that are easier to keep up. This, too, is a decision not to be made on a whim. The house may have more meaning to you and to your children than you realize.

But if you sell and "trade down" to a smaller unit, the profit you make on the sale can go a long way toward providing additional financial security in your non-working years. (People over age sixty-five pay reduced capital gains taxes, an important consideration if you sell your home.)

Some retirees say there is a pyschological advantage to moving to a new area if you must lower your standard of living because of a reduced retirement income.

"We stayed where we were for a while," says Max Hall of Syracuse, N.Y. "Then it got to be a problem. Friends were always inviting us over to dinner, and we found it difficult to reciprocate. They probably didn't expect us to, but we felt that it was necessary. We got so that it was awkward to accept the invitations from our working friends. We moved into another neighborhood, and the problem was solved. When we moved, no one asked any questions. They might notice the kind of car we drive, but that's about as far as it goes. We found it was the best thing for us to do. We still have our friends and the other things that we've enjoyed for years, but the pressure is off."

If you are moving into new quarters—in your home town or elsewhere—here are some possibilities you will want to consider:

MOBILE HOMES

Some Americans still recoil at the thought of living in a so-called mobile home, because they relate the term only to the mobile-home shantytowns that still mar the landscapes on the fringes of some cities.

But mobile homes today have not only become respectable, many mobile-home communities are downright luxurious. And Americans by the millions are finding them an answer to retirement living, particularly with the escalating cost of conventional housing. Some six million Americans now live in mobile homes, most of which cost less than $20,000, excluding the land.

The eight leading states for mobile home living, according to Woodall's Mobile Home Park Directory, are California, Florida, Texas, Michigan, Arizona, Illinois, Ohio and Washington. They are prevalent in most of the United States except the Northeast. Vance Packard wrote in "A Nation of Strangers" that if all the mobile homes in Florida were hitched end-to-end they would make a solid line from Florida to California.

These dwellings are more appropriately called "modular" homes, because they often rest on permanent foundations, have no wheels and are about as mobile as a concrete bunker. They are usually made of wood with an enameled metal coating. In areas where hurricanes are a threat, the homes are usually tied down with cables. Several mobile-home modules are often combined to make sizable homes.

Mobile homes aren't mortgaged in the conventional way. Instead, they are purchased like automobiles, usually with a higher interest rate and a shorter time for the loan to be liquidated. Some owners trade their homes in for new ones after ten years or so, because they become obsolete much faster than conventional houses.

They range in price from $6,000 to $30,000 or more, fully equipped with furniture and major appliances. In most mobile-home parks, you must also pay a rental for the land.

As with anything else, you must investigate carefully before buying a mobile home, especially in an existing park. Some unfortunates have bought mobile homes in parks offering "guaranteed" lifetime rentals of their lots for very small monthly payments, only to discover that the payments go up regularly. They have also found that they have unwittingly signed documents making it almost impossible to sell the mobile home.

There are many reputable mobile-home parks that have a sense of community much like a small town. Many of them are dominated by retirees, and some restrict or prohibit families with small children.

Besides costing less than conventional housing because of the economics of mass production, mobile homes are cheaper to operate generally. Because they are so compact, heating and air-conditioning are more economical.

But you'll do well to investigate such things as the history of land-rental increases, the availability of proper sewage and garbage disposal and the adequacy of the foundation and anchorage, especially in hurricane areas.

A CASE HISTORY

Let's look at the experience of one satisfied mobile-home owner:

Willa Mason, a native of New Jersey and a widow, has retained the family home in New Jersey but for eleven years has spent her winters in a mobile home in Florida. She maintains a large mobile home in the Buckingham Club Mobile Home Park near Sarasota.

The park isn't far from shopping areas, and is landscaped with shrubbery, palms and tall pines. Traffic in the park is restricted, and solicitors are forbidden. Homeowners are required to maintain gardens. And there is a large clubhouse with a heated swimming pool and shuffleboard courts.

"I never thought that I would end up living in a trailer," Mrs. Mason says, "Up North, we thought they were crummy. But when I saw this, I bought it the same day. It's beautiful and just exactly what I need."

But before finding her mobile home, Mrs. Mason looked at condominiums, villas and single-family houses. A mobile home, she concluded, represented a good compromise between the condominium apartment and a detached house.

"This is like a separate house," she said. "I have lovely neighbors, but they aren't too close. They're near enough to help out if there's any kind of emergency, but not close enough to be a nuisance."

Mrs. Mason's mobile home contains 860 square feet of living space. The walls are paneled with pecan, the floors are carpeted, the kitchen contains a full-size stove and oven and dishwasher, and there are two bedrooms and two-and-a-half baths. She has a carport for her auto and three-wheel bike. The home, completely furnished, cost $12,500, although she replaced some of the furnishings.

The living space is deceptively large. In the living room are a couch, three chairs, end tables, coffee tables and a small desk. A dining area contains a table that can open up to seat twelve. Mrs. Mason said she spends little time on housework because the home is so compact and well-organized.

Like the other residents of the park, Mrs. Mason leases the land on which her mobile home is located. When she first moved there eleven years ago, the yearly lease was $500, but this has since been increased to $1,000. That includes the rent for the lot, daily trash pick-up, street maintenance, water and sewer, use of the clubhouse, swimming pool, and other rec-reational facilities, plus the salary for a resident manager. Homeowners themselves pay no property taxes.

"Where else could I live in Florida for that kind of money?" she asks. "It would cost much more in any other type of housing. Not one of the apartments that I looked at had a living room as large as mine." Some people have screened patios, but I preferred to have it all enclosed as living space. I find it too hot to sit outside, but a lot of people enjoy it."

The highest monthly electrical bill Mrs. Mason has ever had was $50. Usually, it is around $30 or even lower. The outside is cleaned by a professional once a year, which costs $100. The homeowner insurance policy for the mobile home is $119 annually. People sometimes have the outside of the mobile homes repainted by a professional, but in the eleven years Mrs. Mason has owned her home she has not had this expense. It costs about $50 every two years to have the roof maintained to prevent water leakage.

Mrs. Mason enjoys the social life at the community's club-house. She teaches painting classes, free of charge, and there are regular bridge tournaments and poker and bingo games. On holidays, large social gatherings are held at the clubhouse, usually with a band. Once a month, there is a large party so that any new residents can meet their new neighbors.

"Most of the people here get along very well," she says. "We're all retired, so we have a lot in common. Most of the residents were teachers, professors and other professional people. They're very thoughtful and considerate, down-to-earth type of people. We share rides to the shopping centers and that sort of thing. I don't have to live here, but this is what I like."

The Buckingham Club has a homeowner's association to allow residents to present their complaints or suggestions to be relayed to the park owner. A set of rules is enforced by the owner of the park with the recommendations of the residents taken into consideration.

Mrs. Mason stays in her mobile home for six months out of the year, as most of the other residents do. When she wants to have it closed up, the manager does it for her. A month before she returns from New Jersey, she telephones, and the manager opens it for her.

"He turns on the gas, the water and electricity for me," she says. "Usually, he even makes ice and has that in the freezer when I arrive. There's absolutely no fuss or bother on my part."

Although solicitors aren't allowed in the park, the residents do permit fresh produce to be sold there. Twice a week, strawberry and tomato vendors arrive to sell their goods, for example. They set up shop near the clubhouse.

Trips are also organized frequently. The residents charter buses and go to other states quite often on vacations. They also get together for group cruises. There is at least one trip a week to a dinner theater, concert or some type of sports activity.

"There's something going on all the time," Mrs. Mason says. "I went on a trip to Key West and think it's the only way to go. We have a good time on the bus and don't have to worry about driving. It also helps to bring us closer together to create a feeling of community."

SOME SADDER EXPERIENCES

While Mrs. Mason has an ideal retirement home, in her view, this is not necessarily true in all cases at mobile-home parks. A few miles from where she lives, the residents of another park had to go to court to settle grievances with the owner. The residents finally won, but it took them two years of bitter fighting. Some of them were so bitter and disillusioned that they sold their mobile homes and moved.

"I just can't hack it any more," said one sixty-seven-year-old widow. "I'm afraid and I'm tired. The place has lost the feeling of home for me. My husband told me before he died that if I had to sell and take a loss, that's what I should do. I don't want to live here any more. There has been too much bitterness and too many tears."

When residents moved into the mobile-home park, they were required to buy their home from the park owner. They were also told that their rent for the lot would never be more than $20 a month. But they failed to read the fine print. Two years later, the rent had soared to $65 a month and was soon to be raised to $75.

They also discovered that they had to go through the owner's own repair company for work performed on the mobile home. The costs for those repairs were much higher than those of service companies. The owner also had a legal right to do all the yard and ground maintenance, and charged fees the residents thought were exorbitant. Garbage collection was supposed to be free, but residents found themselves paying $2.75 a month for the service.

If they wanted to sell the mobile home, they had to go through the owner and pay a 6 percent commission. They weren't allowed to sell it themselves. When residents bought the homes, the park owner anchored them to cement slabs, effectively preventing them from being moved to another park.

The residents won their suit, but it was a long, bitter and expensive fight. Most of them were disillusioned with the promise of a carefree retirement. Had they read their contracts carefully, they may have been spared their agony.

The attorney general of Florida offers advice for anyone who buys a mobile home: Read your contracts carefully. If you don't understand everything on the documents, consult a lawyer. Otherwise, you might be in for unexpected expense and trouble.

At its best, mobile-home living offers a comfortable and inexpensive dream. At its worst, it can become a nightmare.

CONDOMINIUM LIVING

Like mobile homes, condominiums are not the private preserve of the retired, by any means. Increased costs of single-family homes have prompted millions of Americans to move into multifamily condominium units. The Department of Housing and Urban Development estimates that by 1990, half of our population may be living in condominiums. Most buyers, according to the Urban Land Institute, are in their thirties or forties, but an increasing number of retirees are choosing them for a variety of reasons.

Most people who buy condominiums are attracted by the relatively maintenance-free living. In most condominium developments, a buyer has to join an association that levies maintenance fees to pay to a management company. The rules at condominiums generally permit issuing of a lien against your unit if you fall too far behind in maintenance payments.

The word "condominium" means joint ownership, but buyers of units aren't buying shares in the entire condominium complex necessarily. Sometimes the developer maintains ownership of recreational or other jointly used facilities and even the land on which the condominium unit has been built. There have been instances, particularly in Florida, where developers have charged outrageous rental fees for use of facilities not included in the purchase price.

"A condominium document is a verbal jungle," a lawyer observes. "No one should even think about buying one until the papers are examined by an experienced lawyer."

The declaration of condominium and the sales contract are so complicated that even a guidebook published by the Federal Housing Administration to help you read them runs more than sixty pages. Moreover, all condominium documents are different.

Purchasers of condominium units in effect buy the space enclosed by the four walls of their unit. This can be in a high-rise building, cluster housing, or even single-family residences that are located on ground jointly owned by all.

The rules in condominiums often strictly regulate such things as whether you can have a dog, where to walk your dog, whether you can hang clothing out to dry, where to park your automobile and whether you are allowed to rent your unit to another family.

The restrictions in a well-operated condominium complex are not so arbitrary as to make life unbearable. The rules are usually set by the owners association to protect the style of living. But you should make certain you know the rules and can live with them.

A 1976 survey of condominium owners said most would never go back to a single-family home. The owners enjoyed not having maintenance chores, they felt they could buy more for their money in a condominium, and they enjoyed the recreational facilities.

The first condominium in the United States was built in 1958 by Sidney Colen, a land developer in St. Petersburg, Fla., who said he didn't want his elderly parents to be bothered with maintenance work. The concept has since been refined considerably.

Many condominium complexes offer the residents a wide range of leisure facilities—swimming pools, tennis courts, shuffleboard, saunas, gymnasiums, and even golf courses. There can also be social events and educational classes sponsored by recreation committees. Some complexes include shopping areas.

Aside from the cost of such amenities, the purchase price of a condominium is generally below the cost of a comparable single-family home. William Becker, a housing consultant in Paramus, N.J., says that a family can purchase the same living space for $32,000 in a condominium complex that would cost $40,000 in a detached house. In addition, the condominium buyer often receives the use of recreational facilities.

Based on the expenses in his area, Becker gives a breakdown of costs comparing the $32,000 condominium unit to the $40,000 house. A 10 percent down payment would be $800 less for the condominium purchaser. The monthly expenses from then on, he says, are:

	House	Condominium
Principal and interest	$302	$242
Taxes	100	60
Maintenance and recreation	108	50
Total	$510	$352

According to Becker's figures, the monthly saving by owning a condominium is $158 a month on those items alone. But savings are also realized in utilities and in the amount of work it takes to keep a condominium unit operating. In a detailed study of condominium living, the Environmental Protection Agency noted that the work you have to do at a detached house is 33 percent higher than at a condominium. The EPA also noted savings in heating bills because condominiums have common walls that help insulate the units.

This was how the monthly expenses compared between a comparable condominium and detached house in Sarasota, Fla., by one estimate:

	Single-family home	Condominium
Electricity	$80	$50
Water & sewer	37	20
Lawn care	50	0
Outside Painting	15	0
Hazard Insurance	15	0
Liability Insurance	5	0
Maintenance Fee:	0	50
Total:	$202	$120

Not only did the condominium owners have expenses $82 a month less than the residents of the detached home, but they didn't have to spend time working in the yard. The saving in money and effort can be appealing to many retirees.

Unlike a mobile home, which depreciates in value over the years, a condominium's value tends to go up, and you have practically the same tax advantages for condominium units as those allowed for detached homes.

Unfortunately, unscrupulous developers and sharp salesmen are sometimes involved in the condominium trade. Unknowing buyers have been tied to long-term maintenance leases that have cost them much more than they expected. In some cases the maintenance fees have increased more than 200 percent in a year or two. Not only have purchasers been deluded into thinking they owned the land and recreational facilities, but some have been promised facilities that never materialized.

A person who wants to buy a condominium should exercise due caution. Among the steps suggested in "The Condominium Book," published by Dow Jones Books:

1. Have a lawyer read your declaration of condominium and sales documents. After you sign, you are bound to live with all the stipulations.

2. Check with other owners to see how the building is maintained, what the fees are, and whether the association functions well.
3. Don't make a down payment on a condominium unless you are sure the money goes into an escrow account. If it doesn't and the developer later goes bankrupt, you may lose your money.
4. Make certain that the developer is bound, in writing, to providing the amenities promised by the salesmen.
5. Check with other owners to see whether the construction is sound.
6. Make certain you understand the restrictions and whether you can live with them. If they are too strict, you might find that your life will be too regimented.

Well-designed condominiums have provided residents with a less-expensive way to live. They sometimes can have country-club recreational facilities that the residents might not otherwise be able to afford. The physical work involved in maintaining a condominium is relatively minimal, and so is the monthly living expense. Most people who have found condominium developments that are soundly planned and managed enjoy a relatively carefree, comfortable life. For a retiree, who might want to devote effort to things other than yard work and maintenance, they can be ideal.

SPECIAL CASES

Retirees who live on low incomes, or who are semi-invalids, often have special housing needs. There are several federal programs aimed at providing what they need at a price they can afford. Some of these housing programs are still in the experimental stages, but they do hold promise for the future.

The Housing and Urban Development Acts of 1970 and 1974 include provisions to encourage the development of residential settings for older people, including those who are handicapped or disabled. Since 1956, over 600,000 dwellings have been developed to provide low-cost housing for the elderly. But there is a long waiting list for this housing, and housing authorities often have the unhappy task of having to evict tenants who can no longer care for the premises.

"Public-housing agencies are faced with the fact that either they must evict the more frail or impaired who cannot sustain the shopping, cooking or heavy housekeeping chores designed for the hale and hearty, or they must develop—on a crash and perhaps ill-founded basis—some semblance of the services these aging occupants need to maintain at least semi-independence in a residential setting," Marie McGuire Thompson, a housing specialist with the International Center for Social Gerontology in Washington, D.C., told Congress.

An experimental form of housing that is proving successful in a number of locations is "congregate" living facilities. These housing units are designed specifically for semi-independent retirees who may need help with heavy housekeeping and cooking and the companionship of other people, but who don't require the services of a nursing home.

Congregate housing may be campus-type facilities, small cooperative housing projects or boarding homes organized and operated by the retirees themselves. For lower-income families, HUD describes congregate housing as: "a residential environment which includes services, such as meals, housekeeping, health, personal hygiene and transportation, which are required to assist impaired, but not ill, elderly tenants to maintain or return to a semi-independent life style and avoid institutionalization as they grow older."

In short, congregate housing, whether it is subsidized by the government or operated by the retirees themselves, is a living arrangement that delays institutionalization for older people. A study by the U.S. General Accounting Office in 1975 discovered that most people who were living in expensive nursing homes, mental hospitals or homes for the elderly, really didn't belong there. They simply had no other alternative.

WHERE TO LIVE, WHAT TO LIVE IN

The study, involving nearly 400 patients in Michigan, concluded that almost 80 percent did not require skilled nursing care. A 1971 study of New York City medical patients in nursing homes conducted by the state comptroller's office found that from 53 to 61 percent of the patients did not need to be there. In Cleveland, the head of the nursing-home Medicaid program put the proportion of patients unnecessarily in homes under her jurisdiction at 90 percent.

Dr. Wilma Donahue, director of the International Center for Social Gerontology, claims that more than 3 million older persons in the United States need to live in housing where at least some of their needs are cared for. Of these, she says 2.4 million could live in congregate housing, as an alternative to nursing homes if such housing were available.

The U.S. Department of Housing and Urban Development started four pilot congregate housing projects as part of the public-housing program several years ago, and they have been remarkably successful. Similar housing facilities for the elderly are going up throughout the country, many operated by nonprofit organizations offering very low rentals.

Two congregate public housing developments in Toledo and Columbus, Ohio, not only provide accommodations for former nursing-home patients, but for others who had been placed in state mental institutions. The state assumed responsibility for constructing and operating both facilities, and actually saved money by collecting rents from residents instead of paying to have them institutionalized.

The International Center for Social Gerontology, a nonprofit research organization, has been conducting studies that underscore the need for some kind of national congregate housing program.

"Adding years to life but depriving the elderly of the opportunity to remain active in society to the fullest extent of their capacities creates self-pity, apathy and despair among many older people," says Dr. Marie McGuire Thompson. "It also robs the community of the presence and contributions of its most experienced citizens."

The Department of Housing and Urban Development has also authorized several million dollars to be used to convert inner-city buildings into low-rent housing for the elderly. The central locations are close to services and public transportation.

One such project is the Philadelphia Geriatric Center, a nonprofit complex that provides housing for the elderly and treats those who are suffering from physical and mental handicaps that make them dependent on others. The center is just a few blocks from the subway. At the center's six-acre campus is a nursing home with 330 beds and an eleven-story project with 176 efficiency apartments for elderly people who are in good health.

A housing specialist for HUD calls such projects "a boon to many elderly needing decent housing in an independent arrangement." He adds that the projects "can provide a buffer to the loneliness that so often accompanies old age."

If you are looking for retirement housing, you will do well to anticipate the certainty that you won't always be in the pink of health.

The National Retirement Council suggests this checklist of things to look for in retirement housing for maximum safety, comfort and convenience:

—Are all rooms on one floor, with no walking hazards?

—Are doors and halls wide enough to accommodate a wheelchair?

—Is lighting adequate, especially near any stairways?

—Are there non-slip surfaces in the kitchen and bathroom?

—Are there handrails on any stairways, in bathrooms and in other potentially hazardous places?

—Is there heating and cooling to provide 70-to-75-degree temperatures in each room?

—Is there adequate provision to muffle any outside noises?

—Is there enough space to provide a separate bedroom for sick care, with easy access to a bathroom?

Chapter 9

Take Good Care
of Yourself

Earl J. Becker, who is seventy-six, rises early each morning and jogs around his Florida neighborhood, ending the last few blocks of his two-mile course in a sprint. Several thousand miles away, Charles A. Bush, sixty-three, a retired school superintendent in Illinois, gets up and does thirty minutes of muscle-wrenching calisthenics to start his day.

These two men didn't begin doing their exercises after retirement; they started years ago. If they hadn't, chances are that they would not enjoy the muscle tone and general good health that they do today.

"You're not going to change much when you retire," Bush says. "If you want to be healthy and happy in retirement, you better get started early."

Good health is partly hereditary, but there are things you can do to protect and enhance it. The sooner you begin taking care of your body, the better you will feel, and the healthier you will probably be in retirement.

Heart disease is the number-one killer in America today. Eighty-six percent of all people sixty-five and over die of coronary artery disease, or arteriosclerosis. It is a disease that most doctors think can be forestalled to some degree by diet and exercise, starting in your twenties.

There are no sure-fire paths to good health now or in retirement, but there are three basic rules that doctors say should be followed: eat properly and in moderation, get the

Leading Causes of Deaths in the U.S., 1968

Rank	Cause of death[1]	Number	Rate per 100,000 population in specified group
	45-64 YEARS OF AGE		
	Both sexes		
	All causes	479,038	1,176.0
1	Diseases of heart	181,446	445.4
2	Malignant neoplasms	116,385	285.7
3	Cerebrovascular diseases	32,145	78.9
4	Accidents	23,896	58.7
	Motor vehicle accidents	11,031	27.1
	All other accidents	12,865	31.6
5	Cirrhosis of liver	16,714	41.0
6	Influenza and pneumonia	12,107	29.7
7	Diabetes mellitus	9,982	24.5
8	Bronchitis, emphysema, and asthma	9,856	24.2
9	Suicide	8,374	20.6
10	Homicide	3,190	7.8
	All other causes	64,943	159.4
	Men		
	All causes	309,995	1,586.8
1	Diseases of heart	132,393	677.7
2	Malignant neoplasms	62,876	321.8
3	Cerebrovascular diseases	17,648	90.3
4	Accidents	17,463	89.4
	Motor vehicle accidents	7,802	39.9
	All other accidents	9,661	49.5
5	Cirrhosis of liver	11,039	56.5
6	Influenza and pneumonia	7,849	40.2
7	Bronchitis, emphysema, and asthma	7,593	38.9
8	Suicide	5,893	30.2
9	Diabetes mellitus	4,747	24.3
10	Homicide	2,569	13.2
	All other cases	39,925	204.4
	Women		
	All causes	169,043	797.3
1	Malignant neoplasms	53,509	252.4
2	Diseases of heart	49,053	231.4
3	Cerebrovascular diseases	14,497	68.4
4	Accidents	6,433	30.3
	Motor vehicle accidents	3,229	15.2
	All other accidents	3,204	15.1
5	Cirrhosis of liver	5,675	26.8
6	Diabetes mellitus	5,235	24.7
7	Influenza and pneumonia	4,258	20.1
8	Suicide	2,481	11.7
9	Bronchitis, emphysema, and asthma	2,263	10.7
10	Infections of kidney	1,234	5.8
	All other causes	24,405	115.1

Rank	Cause of death	Number	Rate per 100,000 population in specified group
	65 YEARS AND OVER		
	Both Sexes		
	All causes	1,189,697	6,219.7
1	Diseases of heart	541,457	2,630.7
2	Malignant neoplasms	176,963	925.2
3	Cerebrovascular diseases	172,969	904.3
4	Influenza and pneumonia	47,060	246.0
5	Arteriosclerosis	32,002	167.3
6	Accidents	28,564	149.3
	Motor vehicle accidents	7,570	39.6
	All other accidents	20,994	109.8
7	Diabetes mellitus	26,119	136.5
8	Bronchitis, emphysema, and asthma	21,690	113.4
9	Cirrhosis of liver	6,950	36.3
10	Infections of kidney	6,720	35.1
	All other causes	129,203	675.5
	Men		
	All causes	613,356	7,488.2
1	Diseases of heart	277,890	3,392.6
2	Malignant neoplasms	98,807	1,206.3
3	Cerebrovascular diseases	75,989	927.7
4	Influenza and pneumonia	24,643	300.9
5	Bronchitis, emphysema, and asthma	17,884	218.3
6	Accidents	14,818	180.9
	Motor vehicle accidents	4,827	58.9
	All other accidents	9,991	122.0
7	Arteriosclerosis	13,686	167.1
8	Diabetes mellitus	9,854	120.3
9	Cirrhosis of liver	4,485	54.8
10	Peptic ulcer	3,785	46.2
	All other causes	71,515	873.1
	Women		
	All causes	576,341	5,270.1
1	Diseases of heart	263,567	2,410.1
2	Cerebrovascular diseases	96,980	886.8
3	Malignant neoplasms	78,156	714.7
4	Influenza and pneumonia	22,417	205.0
5	Arteriosclerosis	18,316	167.5
6	Diabetes mellitus	16,265	148.7
7	Accidents	13,746	125.7
	Motor vehicle accidents	2,743	25.1
	All other accidents	11,003	100.6
8	Bronchitis, emphysema, and		
9	asthma	3,806	34.8
10	Infections of kidney	3,475	31.8
	Hypertension	3,117	28.5
	All other causes	56,496	516.6

[1]Causes are categorized according to the Eighth Revision, International Classification of Diseases, Adapted for Use in the United States 1965.

proper exercise, and have regular physical examinations. Diseases such as diabetes and cancer, if detected early with regular check-ups by your doctor, can usually be cured or controlled. Preventive medicine is the best kind.

Of the $60 billion a year spent for health care in the U.S., a fourth is spent by people over sixty-five, either out of their own pockets or from Medicare. The elderly have to visit doctors more frequently than younger people. The average person under forty-five visits his doctor four times a year. That increases to an average of six visits annually for those over sixty-five.

Even so, Dr. Anthony Lenzer, associate professor of public health and human development at the University of Hawaii, says that older Americans are actually quite healthy. Dr. Lenzer defines health as the ability to function well enough to carry out normal life roles and responsibilities. By that standard, he says, retired Americans are in good shape. Only 5 percent of the Americans who are over sixty-five are ill enough to live in nursing homes, homes for the aged, mental hospitals or other such institutions. The National Center for Health Statistics reports that even at age eighty-five, eight out of ten people are still able to care for themselves.

EATING RIGHT

Many diseases, from arteriosclerosis to diabetes, are related at least partially to what we eat and how our body handles it. There are dozens of diet books on the market that claim to tell you how to save your life, how to stay young, how to eat fat and grow thin, and so forth. Many doctors and nutritionists refer to these as "fad" diets and warn you to avoid them. Instead, good, sensible eating habits are important now and as you get older.

Government nutritional experts Geraldine M. Piper and Emily M. Smith point out that the eating habits of older people "represent a lifetime record which has been influenced by multiple environmental, emotional and physiological factors." It's a good idea, then, to form proper eating habits while you are still young.

Consult your doctor about a proper diet. Most Americans are at least a few pounds overweight, and it is a dangerous condition that puts undue stress on the heart, arteries, pancreas, liver and other organs of the body. These vital organs get enough wear and tear as it is, without adding to the burden with excess baggage.

Nutritionists Smith and Piper say that the daily diet should include good-quality protein from animal sources such as milk, cheese, meat, eggs, fish and poultry, as well as whole grains, dried beans and peas and nuts. You also need green and yellow vegetables, ruffage such as salads or raw vegetables, and fruits.

Instead, how many of us opt for a piece of pie and a cup of black coffee for lunch? Or load down our plates with potatoes and gravy, eliminating vegetables? Sooner or later,the excessive intake of fats and starches catches up with us.

Your body's nutritional needs do not change as you grow older, but you may need less food, depending on your physical condition and degree of activity. Because they tend to slow down, older people don't need as much food as an 18-year-old who runs at full steam most of the time. With age, there is a gradual reduction in the body's metabolic rate. The digestive processes slow down,and food is not absorbed as well.

A study by the National Institutes of Health showed that nearly every person over the age of sixty needed to revise his eating habits. Other reports have emphasized that health counseling and nutritional guidance are almost necessities for most older people, who often don't eat as they should.

Several obstacles stand in the way of proper nutrition for the elderly, NIH notes. For one thing, they often don't have enough money to buy the types of foods they need to stay healthy. Their appetites decrease with age, and reduced activity, fatigue and weakness—or simply living alone—deprives them of the incentive to eat well.

Dieticians say that eating plans developed for diabetics,

available from your family doctor or local health department, provide a good basic diet for most people. This list not only tells you what kinds of foods to eat, but it tells you how much you can have to provide you with a given number of calories each day.

Dr. Gerald Bumper, a dietician with the Executive Nuclear Laboratory in Bradenton, Fla., prefers to remain fifteen pounds under his recommended weight because it makes him lighter on his feet, gives him more stamina and reduces the work on his heart. Bumper eats raw cereal with honey and skim milk for breakfast, a bag of peanuts or soybeans for lunch, plus six ounces of meat, potatoes, rice or bread, a salad and fruit for dinner.

Compared with the way most Americans eat, that constitutes a starvation diet, but Dr. Bumper is an active man who often works twelve hours a day and he says he has all the energy and nutrients he needs to stay well.

The average American eats 3,500 calories a day," Dr. Bumper says, "and for most people that's about 1,500 calories too many. Only people who are doing physically strenuous work, like dock workers or construction laborers, need that many calories. The average Japanese has 1,500 calories a day, and I've never seen a fat Japanese. And the incidence of death by heart attack is very low compared to this country."

Physical changes that occur when we grow older reduce the number of calories we need. With age, there is a gradual reduction in the body's metabolic rate, the digestive processes slow down, and food is not absorbed as well as in youth because of reduced digestive enzymes. Our nutritional balance remains the same, however. And balance is the key. Nutritionists say we need foods from these basic groups each day: milk, meat, fruits and vegetables, bread and cereals.

Proper diet may be even more important to our good health and length of life than we now know. In two separate experiments, research scientists have lengthened the life of mice and monkeys by decreasing the amount of food they ate. Nothing else. Instead of letting the animals eat what they

106

Desirable Weights

MEN AGE 25 AND OVER

Weight in pounds according to frame (in indoor clothing)

HEIGHT (WITH SHOES ON) Feet	Inches	SLENDER FRAME	MEDIUM FRAME	LARGE FRAME
5	2	112-120	118-129	126-141
5	3	115-123	121-133	129-144
5	4	118-126	124-136	132-148
5	5	121-129	127-139	135-152
5	6	124-133	130-143	138-156
5	7	128-137	134-147	142-161
5	8	132-141	138-152	147-166
5	9	136-145	142-156	151-170
5	10	140-150	146-160	155-174
5	11	144-154	150-165	159-179
6	0	148-158	154-170	164-184
6	1	152-162	158-175	168-189
6	2	156-167	162-180	173-194
6	3	160-171	167-185	178-199
6	4	164-175	172-190	182-204

WOMEN AGE 25 AND OVER

Weight in pounds according to frame (in indoor clothing)

HEIGHT (WITH SHOES ON) Feet	Inches	SLENDER FRAME	MEDIUM FRAME	LARGE FRAME
4	10	92-98	96-107	104-119
4	11	94-101	98-110	106-122
5	0	96-104	101-113	109-125
5	1	99-107	104-116	112-128
5	2	102-110	107-119	115-131
5	3	105-113	110-122	118-134
5	4	108-116	113-126	121-138
5	5	111-119	116-130	125-142
5	6	114-123	120-135	129-146
5	7	118-127	124-139	133-150
5	8	122-131	128-143	137-154
5	9	126-135	132-147	141-158
5	10	130-140	136-151	145-163
5	11	134-144	140-155	149-168
6	0	138-148	144-159	153-173

Source: U.S. Department of health, Education and Welfare, and Office of Education.

would have eaten under natural conditions, the scientists forced them to live only on foods they provided. The result was, in both tests, that the life expectancy of the control animals increased by one-third.

"Excessive eating and the consumption of too much junk food are probably the biggest problems in American nutrition," a dietician says. "Unfortunately, most people don't take the time to eat right, and it's hard to break the habit. You see people who get to be thirty and they've already gone to pot."

A common dietary failing among older people is that they don't eat enough protein. Most of their calories come from starches and sugars. No matter how old you are, you could benefit from an examination of your eating habits. If you eat a balanced diet, there will be no need for you to take vitamins to remain healthy, unless they are prescribed by your doctor.

IMPORTANCE OF EXERCISE

One of the things many people forget in this age of labor-saving machinery is that the human body is made to move. We sit at desks, ride elevators, and are whisked around to and fro in buses, airplanes, automobiles and trains.

Dr. William Haskell, a heart specialist at Stanford University, says that even a busy housewife should walk at least one mile a day. Most of us hear this kind of advice regularly but tend to ignore it. The muscles and joints become stiff and deteriorate when they aren't used. In an unusual experiment a few years ago, a group of college students wanted to show how inactivity affects the body. Each of the students was placed in a plaster body cast for several weeks so that he couldn't even move his toes. When the casts were removed, the students could barely walk, their muscles were flabby and their joints were stiff.

Other, less obvious things were happening internally. Their hearts and vascular systems didn't work as well as before. There was a distinct loss of calcium in the bones, making them brittle and more apt to break. Their muscles had deteriorated, losing strength and becoming flabby, and the joints were not flexible. When they moved they tired quickly. Although they had been in the casts for just a few weeks, it took them several months of concentrated effort to get back in peak shape.

Unfortunately, too many people make the mistake of getting their exercise only on weekends. To stay healthy, a person should exercise moderately every day. The high incidence of heart attacks during the winter snow-shoveling season is clear evidence of how sudden, taxing exercise when you are out of shape can be fatal. Regular exercise, in moderation, is the key.

Dr. Edwin Smith, of the University of Michigan's physical medicine and rehabilitation department, says that with just a little exercise, a person can stay in good condition. For older people, he suggests such activities as golf, hiking, hunting, gardening, or working on the house. Besides keeping the body in good working order, such activities have psychological advantages by releasing tensions and working off steam in a constructive way, Dr. Smith says.

People who have developed good exercise habits earlier in life find it easier to keep fit later in life. Admiral John S. McCain Jr. is such a man. At one time, Admiral McCain was the commander of the Atlantic Fleet Amphibious Training Center in Little Creek, Va. A short, nervous man, McCain seems to be constantly in motion. He also is an avid jogger and a fierce tennis player.

Recently, at age fifty-two, he entered a tennis tournament, worked his way into the finals and ultimately defeated a twenty-year-old for the championship.

"I kept waiting for him to tire," his young opponent said afterwards. "He didn't. I think he could have played five more sets if he had needed to."

But even if your idea of exercise has been walking to the refrigerator for a snack, rather than tennis or jogging, you can still benefit by beginning a modest daily regimen of exercise.

Take the case of Dr. Christian Amoroso, an internist from Longmont, Colo. In his mid-thirties, Dr. Amoroso took stock of himself and especially his waistline, expanded by the kind of sedentary lives many of us lead. "Physician, heal thyself," he said to himself.

For starters, he decided to jog a mile. But after three-quarters of a mile he had to stop. His heart was pounding like a pile-driver, and he had a stabbing pain in his side.

Amoroso threw himself enthusiastically into an exercise program and by the end of a year, he could run a mile in less than eight minutes. Pacing himself, he could run for three miles. Five years from the time he realized how out-of-shape he'd become, Amoroso had completed the grueling Boston Marathon, had run up 14,264-foot Mt. Evans, Colorado's tallest mountain, and had run up and down 14,110-foot Pikes Peak.

The once-pudgy physician dropped from 195 pounds to 160 pounds, and he feels much better—physically and mentally—than he did five years ago. "My sights are different," he says. "Physically, I'm not frightened by much, and mentally I'll take on all sorts of things. Being in shape changes your perspective. 'I can't do it' becomes 'I can do anything.' "

You may be beyond the time when you can hope to seriously challenge a twenty-year-old in a tennis tournament or conquer Pikes Peak, but a program of exercise can still help improve not only your health outlook but also your sense of well-being.

With the medical advances of past decades, lengthening the life expectancy of Americans almost miraculously, many health authorities believe most future miracles will have to be initiated by the people themselves.

Dr. John H. Knowles, president of the research-oriented Rockefeller Foundation, was quoted in *The Wall Street Journal:* "The individual must realize that a perpetuation of the present system of high-cost, after-the-fact medicine will only result in higher costs and more frustration. The next major advance in the health of the American people will result only from what the individual is willing to do for himself."

LEARNING TO RELAX

Just as important as proper food and exercise is a proper emotional outlook. As we suggested earlier, retirement can bring psychological stress beyond reckoning.

Of course, it's much easier to *say* you must learn to deal with stress than to actually *do* it. You can develop an exercise program to keep physically fit, but how can you develop defenses against emotional stress?

Attitudes towards stressful situations are usually developed early in life, but it is possible to alter them. Scores of books and articles have been written about so-called biofeedback techniques of controlling anxiety—and even lowering blood pressure without the aid of drugs.

Many doctors now contend that stress can contribute to diabetes, ulcers, kidney disease and heart attacks, as well as depression. Stress has also been shown to increase the pain of arthritis. In short, stress tends to hit you wherever you are vulnerable.

Drs. Meyer Friedman and Ray H. Roseman refer to the "hurry sickness" that comes from crowding too much activity into our lives. But this can be easier to cope with, by simply cutting back on the activity, than the stresses that often afflict retirees. Retirees are especially susceptible to symptoms of stress if they haven't developed interests and activities to keep their minds and bodies occupied after leaving the workaday life behind.

Dr. Daniel J. Levinson, a psychologist at Yale University, says it behooves retirees to develop interests to minimize stress. For those who need other help in dealing with stress, Dr. William A. Nolen suggests routines such as yoga, meditation, self-hypnosis, breathing exercises and other such crutches that many find useful.

In discussing the "retirement syndrome" in his prize-winning book, "Why Survive? Growing Old in America," Dr. Robert N. Butler says there is a lot of mythology on the subject, but he acknowledges that some otherwise healthy people develop headaches, gastrointestinal symptoms, irritability, nervousness and lethargy associated with retirement.

If additional stressful situations are superimposed on the retiree, such as moving to a new home or the death of a friend or close relative, the effects can be devastating.

Drs. T.H. Homes and R.H. Rahe conducted a study to rate the stress-causing events in our lives. They developed this list, ranking the events in order of the stress they cause:

LIFE EVENT	MEAN VALUE
1. Death of a spouse	100
2. Divorce	73
3. Marital separation	65
4. Jail term	63
5. Death of close family member	63
6. Personal injury or illness	53
7. Marriage	50
8. Fired at work	47
9. Marital reconciliation	45
10. Retirement	45
11. Change in health of family member	44
12. Pregnancy	40
13. Sex difficulties	39
14. Gain of new family member	39
15. Business readjustment	39
16. Change in financial state	38
17. Death of close friend	37
18. Change to different line of work	36
19. Change in number of arguments with spouse	35
20. Mortgage over $10,000	31
21. Foreclosure of mortgage or loan	30
22. Change in responsibilities at work	29
23. Son or daughter leaving home	29
24. Trouble with in-laws	29
25. Outstanding personal achievement	28
26. Wife beginning or stopping work	26
27. Beginning or ending school	26

Note that retirement ranks tenth on the list. The doctors found that those with the greatest number of stress points in the shortest time are candidates for illness. If you have accumulated 200 to 300 points in their mean-value ratings in the past twelve months, they calculate, you have a better-than-average chance of getting a stress-related illness within the next twelve months.

Of course, we can't avoid stress completely—and probably wouldn't if we could. Dr. Hans Selye of the University of Montreal calls stress "the spice of life," as it prompts us to do things we otherwise might avoid. But, as with many of the spices of life for the not-so-young, a little stress can go a long way.

Chapter 10

New Work for Old Hands

Gladys M. Sprinkle was sitting at her desk in Montgomery County, Md., when a fifty-six-year-old man came in with a familiar problem. He had lost his job and was unable to find anyone who would employ him.

Mrs. Sprinkle, the energetic director of the Over-Sixty Counseling and Employment Service of the Montgomery County Federation of Women's Clubs, went to work right away, although the client in this case was under sixty. The first thing she had to do was find out all she could about him.

"Individualized counseling is important to each applicant," she says. "This involves listening—listening—and listening—to the whole person."

The fifty-six-year-old man was an engineer, unemployed for many months, who was living on welfare. Doors had been slammed in his face because of his age, even though it was never stated as a reason.

"This is subtle discrimination in action," Mrs. Sprinkle says. "The kind we can't legally pursue."

Mrs. Sprinkle's office maintains an information bank on current labor-market trends, and she knew that there had to be a job available for an engineer. She developed thirty-eight possibilities. After her organization "pried open some doors," she says, the engineer was finally given a job paying $21,600 a year.

Age discrimination in employment practices is illegal. Federal law states that anyone up to age sixty-five must be given the same consideration of a job as is given to any other applicant. Before this legislation was passed, thousands of men and women over forty-five were refused jobs because of their ages. Enforcement of this law is relatively new, and the problem still persists. What has happened, Mrs. Sprinkle says, is that "age discrimination has gone underground."

Jobs are available for retirees, but they are usually low-paying and difficult to find. Organizations like the one headed by Mrs. Sprinkle are scattered throughout the country to help.

Many retirees want to work if for no other reason than to keep involved. The Roper poll in 1977 showed 61 percent of Americans would like a part-time job after retirement. A poll by Louis Harris in 1974 found that four of ten persons over age sixty-four would like to work, either for pay or as volunteers.

The U.S. Census Bureau reported in 1975 that more than 2.5 million Americans over age sixty-five were working for money. That figure included people who hadn't retired and those who retired and decided they wanted to return to work.

Mrs. Carolyn Millard, an officer with the Senior Adult Counseling and Employment Service in Arlington County, Va., told a congressional committee that if unemployment statistics counted all the people who had been forced to retire because of age but who still wanted to work, the figures would rise by at least two percentage points.

White-collar, middle-level executives have the most difficulty finding jobs during retirement. They are often told that they are overqualified for the jobs—usually menial—for which they apply to subsidize their pension and Social Security incomes.

"All my badges of success are now my liabilities," a fifty-six-year-old executive laments.

Still, there are a great many part-time jobs available. Ordinarily, the low salary and short hours aren't of concern to retirees because they can't earn more than $4,000 a year without jeopardizing their Social Security payments. Part-time work can be highly satisfying, even though the skills required may be far below the retiree's capabilities.

Thanks to the work being done by employment centers specializing in the placement of people over fifty, many employers are finding it to their advantage to hire retirees, because they will work cheaply.

"This isn't taking away jobs the younger ones might do," Mrs. Millard says. "Most senior citizens have income aside from what they earn through us. The jobs available to them are service jobs, and a lot of younger people don't like that kind of work. They feel it is not up to their status. They want something with a future. They want to look ahead to promotions. These are dead-end jobs."

Yet statistics show that retirees make good employees. They are much more likely to show up for work early, miss fewer days and leave the job later than younger people. A national effort, sponsored by the federal government, is being conducted to place older people in jobs and to educate employers.

Martha Fletcher, an Arlington, Va., employment specialist for older Americans, has interviewed retirees seeking jobs in nearly all skills and professions. Many have found jobs that are closely related to their specialty, although they usually have had to take a severe cut in salary and work fewer hours.

Some of the jobs retirees have found through Ms. Fletcher's office:

A courier who had worked for a dental laboratory and a construction company became a driver. A former mutual-fund salesman took a job as a telephone solicitor for an insurance company. A former government clerk went to work as a clerk in a hardware store. A retired legal secretary took temporary part-time work. A former professional man does grounds-maintenance chores. A clerk-typist became a canvasser for a health-care project.

Retirees willing to give up their Social Security benefits entirely to find full-time employment often find that employers aren't anxious to hire a person over sixty-two, no matter how well-qualified he may be.

117

"TWO-FOR-ONE" CONCEPT

Several employment centers for retirees have come up with the concept of "two for one," or the hiring of two part-time retirees for one job. This gives two retirees jobs at a salary that doesn't affect their Social Security benefits, and provides the employer with the manpower he needs.

Once in a while, a retiree finds a part-time job that blossoms into something beyond his expectations. A former public-relations man in Arlington, Va., was referred to a part-time job at a men's club that eventually resulted in a promotion to senior adult supervisor. Then, he became editor of the county's senior-citizen newsletter.

An interior designer who had been reluctant to hire a person over sixty years old was happy after she did. "She's the best worker I've ever had," the employer says. "She's never late, gets along well with everyone, and is the most conscientious and dependable worker this agency ever had."

Some employers take advantage of the fact that retirees can earn only $4,000 before they start losing Social Security benefits. A senior-citizen employment counselor tells of a dental laboratory that makes a practice of hiring people on Social Security and paying them the minimum wage. When the employes earn their limit, they quit and are replaced by other retirees.

If you want a job in retirement, you might as well forget about going to a profit-making employment agency, as they seldom work with retirees. The Department of Labor urges retirees to contact the state employment offices where they live, the local branch of the Administration on Aging, or a senior employment service in the area. Retirees can find jobs, but they usually have to look longer and harder than younger people, and they must fight the discouragement of being frequently rejected.

"When it comes right down to getting a job, it requires a lot of hard work and many, many calls," says Rep. William J. Randall, chairman of the House Select Committee on Aging.

WORKING FOR YOURSELF

Some retirees choose to work for themselves. J.R. Stancliffe, a former executive with a major shoe-manufacturing company, became bored with retirement and started his own manufacturing firm. Then he expanded into civic work and eventually formed an economic improvement council in southern Florida.

Jim and Ada Irving were in their fifties in 1968 when they sold their business, in Chicago, which supplied equipment to school science laboratories. They bought an apple orchard near Cooksville, Ill., even though they knew nothing about apples.

The Irvings, profiled in a *National Observer* article, say they welcomed early retirement as an opportunity to move to the country. And their business has been so successful that they started a gourmet-food and gift shop complete with a mail-order catalog.

Jim Irving is quite pleased with the "retirement" venture. He rails against the idea that retirement has to be "some sort of pre-burial experience." He says, "At a certain age, you're put on a shelf, and society tells you that you've lost your potential." That can be a self-fulfilling prophecy that an aging person must resist, he says.

Frank Blair, who reported the news on the "Today" show until he retired, maintains his contacts with television and sometimes makes commercials. Blair, who used to be at work at 4 a.m., now says he sleeps until about 9, so that he doesn't get to see "Today" any longer. "Frankly," he says, "I don't like to get up that early."

One retiree who wanted to have something to do with his free time was persuaded by his wife to start a tool-rental business. He had a garage full of expensive garden tools, saws and drills that the younger people in the neighborhood couldn't afford to buy and that he hardly ever used. He began renting them for a small fee.

IS THE PEACE CORPS FOR YOU?

The government has poured several million dollars into programs aimed at creating employment for older Americans. Most of these programs are termed "volunteer" projects because they pay only small stipends.

Some programs, such as the **Peace Corps** and **Volunteers in Service to America (VISTA)**, have previously aimed their recruiting efforts at college dropouts or recent college graduates. Now, they are actively trying to get retirees into the program because, as one VISTA official says, "they've got a lot of experience and a life-time of learning to contribute."

The Peace Corps, though actively recruiting older volunteers, was surprised when Harold and Bertha Soderquist, eighty-one and seventy-seven years of age respectively, applied. To the Soderquists, the Peace Corps seemed to be an opportunity to make their retirement even more exciting than their working years.

Not long ago, they read a newspaper advertisement seeking Peace Corps volunteers. Age was no barrier, so they both applied. Nine months after answering the advertisement, they were in Western Samoa, teaching English and mathematics.

The Soderquists are the oldest married team in the Peace Corps and, although there is no upper limit on age for the program, officials were apprehensive about them. They were accepted tentatively, pending the outcome of interviews, and were transferred from Detroit to Denver for screening. A psychologist minced no words on Mrs. Soderquist.

"What would you do if your husband died over there?" he asked, voicing the fear all of the officials had.

Mrs. Soderquist was unruffled. "Well, I guess we'd have to have him buried," she said.

Mrs. Soderquist says that death is no stranger to people of their ages. It doesn't matter where you die, she says, it matters where and how you live. Mr. and Mrs. Soderquist made a deal with themselves several years ago to keep their lives filled with excitement. They didn't want to stagnate in retirement. They decided that each year they would do something unusual. Their friends either envied them or thought they were crazy.

"There's a certain advantage in being older," Soderquist observes. "You know yourself better—what you can take. You've been through it before and know what to expect of yourself."

GOVERNMENT PROGRAMS

Congress has allocated funds for "volunteer" programs under ACTION, the federal volunteer agency. These programs have been instrumental in helping retirees find work and a sense of purpose that otherwise might have been denied to them.

One of these projects is the **Foster Grandparent Program,** a plan that enables retirees over sixty to supplement their incomes by helping care for children who are physically, emotionally and mentally handicapped. It helps retirees earn additional income in return for performing important tasks. The federal government spends $10.2 million a year on the Foster Grandparent Program, but an independent economic research firm found that its economic benefits outweighed costs by an estimated $1.65 million. For many participants, the rewards of helping a handicapped child improve are at least as important as the small income.

Retirees who join this program may be assigned to an institution, or they can take children into their homes. Foster Grandparents work four hours each day, five days a week with two children who are placed in their care. Besides playing with and amusing the children, they may have specific tasks, such as helping with speech therapy or teaching a child to walk.

Those selected for this program receive forty hours of training by child-care specialists. As soon as they join up, they begin receiving a weekly stipend of $32, transportation allowances, hot meals, accident insurance and free annual physical examinations. In 1975, nearly 13,000 Foster Grandparents were working in 156 locations around the nation.

Ruth Jinks, a Foster Grandparent in Hilo, Hawaii, who has been in the program since it began, describes how it has affected her life: "I have gained much. The children and the grandparents really help each other. They need the tender loving care and we need to feel useful. I have also made new friends, and no longer feel insulated and on the fringe of things."

There are dozens of success stories in the Foster Grandparent Program. A retired typist, for example, helped a severely retarded thirteen-year-old cerebral palsy victim learn how to walk. Another taught a blind and hydrocephalic child to feed himself and talk.

The Foster Grandparent Program has demonstrated the benefits of employing retirees, not only to help them, but also to help society. "Older people have skill, ability and talent to serve their communities and we should take advantage of it," an ACTION spokesman told Congress. Additional information on the program is available from: Foster Grandparent Program, ACTION, 806 Connecticut Avenue, N.W., Washington, D.C. 20525.

A broader ACTION program to find work for retirees over 60 is the **Retired Senior Volunteer Program (RSVP)**. Participants are placed in courts, schools, libraries, day-care centers, hospitals, nursing homes, Boy and Girl Scout offices and other community service centers. Although it is considered a voluntary program, RSVP participants are sometimes paid, on the same scale as those enrolled in the Foster Grandparent program.

At the end of 1975, more than 150,000 retirees were working in various RSVP projects in 666 localities throughout the nation. Volunteers actually get a chance to help other retirees because they often staff senior-citizen centers and other such organizations. They take meals to shut-ins through the Meals on Wheels program or work with the National Nutrition project. The address to write for further information is RSVP Program, ACTION, Washington, D.C. 20525.

New Work for Old Hands

Service Corps of Retired Executives (SCORE) lends special expertise and management assistance to small businesses and community organizations. Benjamin Parker, a Sarasota, Fla., retiree who likes bright Hawaiian print shirts and who drives an automobile with a leopardskin top, spends several days a week helping small businessmen who are just getting started or who are having management problems.

"A lot of guys just need a little bit of information to make things fall in place for them," Parker says. "It's a great feeling to know that you've been able to get them over the hump."

There are more than 200 SCORE chapters and 4,220 volunteers throughout the U.S. Some of its volunteers are paid, but the majority are like Parker: they do it simply because they enjoy helping others and keeping their own minds sharp and active.

Some cities would have a hard time meeting their charitable goals without SCORE's help. The Small Business Administration says that SCORE volunteers have responded to hundreds of thousands of requests for assistance since the program began in 1964.

SCORE volunteers were instrumental in helping administer emergency disaster aid in eastern Pennsylvania after severe flooding in 1972. The organization has also received commendations from Congress for helping with the rehabilitation of former convicts. Information on other activities, chapter locations, and how to join is available from ACTION/SCORE, Washington, D.C. 20525.

Other employment opportunities are available in **VISTA**, which is similar to the Peace Corps except that volunteers do antipoverty work only in the United States and its territories.

The VISTA program has attracted more than 2,500 retired volunteers. They have proved to be such eager workers that VISTA wants, and is getting, more. In 1976, more than 12 percent of all the persons in VISTA were retirees. Another 550 were in training.

The emphasis on attracting skilled retired volunteers is broadening the competence of the organization and is giving meaningful employment to those who need a small income.

Those accepted by VISTA receive training at one of ten training centers lasting a month to a month and a half. They are paid $75 a month from the time they are accepted. When they leave the program, they are paid an additional $50 for each month that they served in VISTA.

In both VISTA and the Peace Corps, retirees mingle with all age groups. Many retirees enjoy working with younger people, and they often can pass on their skills and experience to younger volunteers.

In Idaho, volunteers helped establish basic health-care services to aid senior citizens. Kansas volunteers work with the Meals on Wheels program and staff information centers to help retirees with questions concerning Social Security, Medicare and other aspects of retirement. In Missouri, they are operating a transportation system in a five-county area to get retirees to shopping centers, doctors and other facilities. For additional information, write to VISTA/ACTION, Washington, D.C. 20525.

One thing to remember: Even government workers are subject to the Social Security earnings limitations.

Other programs sponsored by the government of interest to retirees:

Senior Companion Program—Patterned after the Foster Grandparent program, it employs low-income men and women over age sixty to help adults who need special care, such as the handicapped or retarded. Sometimes they work in institutions, but they may also care for a person in their home. More than 1,000 volunteers are working in eighteen such projects. Write to Senior Companion Program/ACTION, 806 Connecticut Ave., N.W., Washington, D.C. 20525.

U.S. Department of Labor Programs—Government sponsored work and training opportunities are available to older Americans under the Comprehensive Employment and Training Act (CETA). The Act, administered by the U.S. Department of Labor, helps the economically disadvantaged of all ages to obtain jobs.

Of special interest to retirees is the section of the law

124

authorizing manpower programs for older workers and special groups such as Indians, migrants, and others who are often handicapped in obtaining employment.

Enrollees, who must be low-income persons fifty-five and over, take part-time jobs provided by local public or private nonprofit agencies. They are paid at least the minimum wage in their areas.

Green Thumb—Sponsored by the National Farmers Union, this limited employment program requires applicants to have a rural or farming background, and they must pass a physical examination. Workers are employed part-time in conservation, beautification, and community-improvement projects in rural areas. They also work in existing community-service agencies or provide special outreach services aiding the aged and handicapped.

Green Thumb conducts an on-the-job training program for workers age forty-five and older under contract with the Labor Department's Manpower Administration.

On-the-job trainees are selected by the employer, who is partially reimbursed by the government for the wages he pays to participants. Write to Green Thumb, Inc., 1012 14th Street, N.W., Washington, D.C. 20005.

Senior Aides—Administered by the National Council of Senior Citizens, this program provides limited employment averaging twenty hours a week in fifty-three urban and rural areas. Aides work in community-service agencies performing a wide variety of jobs, from child care and adult education to home-health and homemaker services. Write to National Council of Senior Citizens, 1511 K Street, N.W. Washington, D.C. 20005.

Senior Community Service Project—Conducted by the National Council on the Aging, this program offers part-time work in a variety of community services in twenty-six urban and rural areas. Aides work in Social Security and state employment-service offices, public housing, libraries, hospitals, schools and in food and nutrition programs of the Administration on Aging and the U.S. Department of Agriculture. They also provide homemaker and home-repair services and outreach services for information and referral centers. Write to National Council on the Aging, 1828 L Street, N.W., Washington, D.C. 20036.

Senior Community Service Employment Program— Sponsored by the National Retired Teachers Association and the American Association of Retired Persons, this program recruits, trains and finds part-time work for people over fifty-five in public or private nonprofit service programs. Community aides work in forty-seven urban and rural areas in a variety of semi-skilled and unskilled jobs, such as clerical positions and building security, and in child-care centers and vocational-educational classes. Write to NRTA/AARP, 1909 K Street, N.W., Washington, D.C. 20006.

Senior Community Service Employment Program— Administered by the Forest Service of the U.S. Department of Agriculture, in cooperation with the U.S. Department of Labor, this program offers employment on the average of three days a week in conservation and beautification projects in twenty-four states. Write to U.S. Department of Agriculture, Forest Service, Washington, D.C. 20250.

Teacher Corps—This program—composed of experienced teachers, who serve as team leaders, and college graduates and undergraduates who serve as interns—is designed to expand and improve educational opportunities for disadvantaged children in urban and rural poverty areas, and to encourage colleges and universities to strengthen their teacher-training programs. Retiree volunteers assist in this effort by serving in local Teacher Corps projects as tutors or instructional assistants. They may serve without compensation, receive hourly wages for work performed, are reimbursed for out-of-pocket expenses, or receive non-monetary compensation—such as academic credit—all depending on arrangements made in local projects. Contact your local school superintendent, or write Teacher Corps, Office of Education, Washington, D.C. 20202.

Adult Basic Education—Adult basic education pro-

126

grams conducted by local public-school systems, community colleges and private nonprofit agencies often enlist retirees as teachers or teacher-aides to help persons over age 16 continue their education and complete at least secondary school. Contact your local school board or the director of adult education in your state department of education. Either can refer you to the appropriate local program.

Census Surveys—The Bureau of Census in the U.S. Department of Commerce maintains a crew of 1,200 to 1,500 part-time interviewers for its current programs and for special surveys. Retirees are eligible. Physical demands in conducting surveys are considerable, and participants should be able to drive a car.

Write the Census Bureau Data Collection Center nearest you. They are located in New York City, Philadelphia, Boston, Atlanta, Dallas, Chicago, Denver, Los Angeles, Seattle, Detroit, Charlotte (N.C.), and Kansas City, Kansas.

Veteran Hospital Volunteers—There is great demand for volunteers to work in the 167 Veterans Administration hospitals throughout the U.S. Service involves such activities as letter writing, errands, reading, feeding patients, and recreation, as well as assisting with admissions, drug treatment, and telephone reassurance programs for patients recently released and confined at home. Meals are sometimes provided. Contact the Chief of Voluntary Service at the VA hospital nearest you.

Federal Job Information Centers—These offices of the U.S. Civil Service Commission, located in more than seventy cities, provide information about federal job opportunities. Generally speaking, there are no upper age limits to federal civil service employment. Persons under age seventy can qualify for regular appointments. Those over seventy are eligible for temporary appointments up to a year, but these can be renewed at the discretion of employers. Contact your local center for details.

There is a vast reserve of talent among America's retirees that is being recognized as a great national resource. One of

127

the most significant moves to date has been made by a consortium of educators and leaders in private industry. This group announced plans to map a $30 million campaign to find ways to use the skills of the elderly. Financed by the Edna McDonnell Clark Foundation, it is the largest nongovernment effort ever undertaken to find ways to capitalize on the talent in America's retiree pool.

"To date, society has looked upon retirement as a dividend of time earned after years of work," the consortium says. "Those who retire in the late 1970s and beyond will be innovators in setting patterns for new, purposeful social roles, for greater involvement in community and civic affairs and for a reappraisal of life goals for work and leisure."

Chapter 11

The Law, Swindlers and the Retiree

When John and Sue Peterson saw a lawyer in New York to have their wills drawn, they felt that they had prepared for any eventuality. Four years later, they moved to Florida, and didn't bother to check their legal situation when they arrived. After John died suddenly, Sue had to contend with a maze of legal complexities amid her grief. The will, which would have been valid in New York, was full of holes under Florida law.

Sue learned the hard way that, no matter where a will is prepared, it will be probated under the laws of the state where a person is residing at the time of his death. States have different probate laws, so it is a good idea to have all legal documents checked if you move out of state.

In Illinois, Bill and Peggy Barkley also believed they had their legal affairs in order. Time passed, and they paid little attention to the changes that were occurring in the state capital. New laws were enacted that invalidated a trust agreement they had prepared to make certain their assets would be equally distributed among their survivors. Both were killed in an automobile accident, and a court fight began between the beneficiaries and the trustees who were to administer the trust. The enormous legal fees exhausted most of the trust once the dispute was settled. And the bitterness that was created among the survivors remains.

Good legal advice is important for retirees or those who are nearing retirement. Virginia Lehmann, who was a staff

129

attorney with the Legal Aid Bureau of United Charities in Chicago for more than twenty years, warns that your margin for error drops as you get older. A working person with years to go before retirement can make a legal mistake and have time to make up for it. But a retiree is stuck.

A survey by the White House Conference on Aging found that fewer than 20 percent of America's retirees get the legal assistance they need. Most of those who were questioned said they felt they needed help from a lawyer, but couldn't afford it. One out of every four retirees also reported that they had been victimized by consumer fraud within the previous year.

Miss Lehmann, author of a booklet entitled, "You, the Law and Retirement," published by the Department of Health, Education and Welfare, says that people should have "family lawyers" just as they have family doctors. That way their lawyer will know them and can familiarize himself with their problems so that he can give better advice when the time comes.

Improper or careless handling of legal matters can create problems for retirees as well as for their survivors. By starting now to get your legal house in order, some of those problems may be eliminated.

THE NEED FOR A WILL

A will is one of the first things most people need and one of the last they get around to taking care of. Who wants to think about death? People who die without wills leave the distribution of their property up to the state. Death without a will can cause long delays in settlement and costly legal fees for the survivors.

Even if you do have a will, that doesn't necessarily mean that you should forget about it. Laws that could affect your property settlement change periodically, sometimes without you being aware of it. Family circumstances often change, too, and when they do, you may need legal advice so that you and your survivors will be protected.

"You should by all means have a new legal checkup whenever there is a major change in your circumstances, such as a death in the family, or a birth, a marriage, divorce, or a change in your family condition," Miss Lehmann says.

Actress Nanette Fabray discovered that there can be problems even if a will has been properly written. A year and a half after the death of her husband, Ronald MacDougall, Miss Fabray was still trying to unravel the legal entanglements concerning their property.

"Once you get past the first shock of losing a loved one, you discover you are living in a new and hostile world," Miss Fabray was quoted as saying. "Instantly after a husband's death, the wife is forced to make decisions that will affect her the rest of her life. Decisions about burial, property taxes, bank accounts, a career. She's expected to make commitments at a time when she is emotionally least able to do so."

For one thing, Miss Fabray could not open their safe-deposit box without an official from the state present. Checks her husband had written were canceled if they had not already cleared the bank. She had to make payments herself. She also ran into problems with inheritance taxes and the disposition of his property.

Lawyers cost money, of course, and when you are on a reduced retirement income, you may be tempted to do what most retirees do: not bother with one. It makes good sense, then, to take care of as many legal matters as possible while you are still working and planning your retirement.

LOW-COST LEGAL ADVICE

You may be able to get low-cost or even free legal advice if you are already retired or if you are at a low income level. The Legal Aid Society in your area can put you in touch with lawyers who volunteer a portion of their time to help those who can't otherwise afford legal assistance. If there is no such organization listed in your telephone directory, you can get the address of the one nearest you by writing to: National Legal Aid and Defender Association, 1155 East 60th Street, Chicago, Ill. 60637.

It is also important to consult a lawyer when you are buying or selling a home. He can help you figure capital-gains taxes on any profit you realize on the sale of a home. If you want to buy or build a new house, a lawyer will go over the contracts and deed and otherwise advise you on legal aspects of the transactions. He'll make certain that you are getting a clear title to the house and property that you are buying.

A lawyer may also give you advice on real estate taxes, and whether they are likely to increase. Developers sometimes make political deals to keep taxes low until the housing development is completed. Soon afterwards, the buyers find to their dismay that the taxes go up.

A lawyer can tell you whether the neighborhood you select is protected by proper zoning. The law will stipulate whether a noisy nightclub or other annoyance can open next door. You should also know about any zoning restrictions that will prevent you from doing some of the things you wish.

Retirees should also consult a lawyer if they are considering moving into a housing development that offers services or care in addition to living quarters, such as retirement communities or hotels, trailer courts, old-age homes, nursing homes, convalescent homes and chronic-illness hospitals.

HINTS ON HOUSING

If your living arrangement is set up on a "pay as you go" basis, you may not need legal advice. However, many living arrangements operate on a prepaid basis and often involve substantial entrance fees. Some even require you to sign over all of your property. Arrangements of this sort should obviously be made with great caution, and only after consulting a lawyer. For your own protection, Miss Lehmann suggests that you specifically investigate these aspects of the housing arrangement:

—What part of the premises you will occupy, whether you are entitled to it for life, and if your privacy will be protected;

—What services and care will you be entitled to and whether there will be an additional charge for it;

—What arrangements are made for medical care and how it will be paid for;

—Whether you are entitled to a refund of all or part of your initial payment if you leave for any reason;

—Whether your rent or other fees can be raised without your consent.

It is also particularly important to know if the enterprise is financially sound. If it isn't, it may not be able to provide you with care in the future. A lawyer can look into the financial and legal details for you.

You can handle your affairs when you are in good health, but what would happen if you become ill? If you are retired, you should designate in advance someone you trust to help out in the event that you become incapacitated. If you plan ahead, it is more likely that things will be taken care of the way you wish.

There are a number of different ways to do this. A lawyer can help you select the way that is best for you depending on your circumstances. He can prepare and look over the documents that confer legal authority to the agent of your choice. Before entering into any of these agreements, get a lawyer's advice.

JOINT OWNERSHIP AND TRUSTS

One method is to place all your assets in joint ownership or joint control. That enables the other party to act for you if you cannot. But joint ownership or control can be tricky. The legal implications depend upon the exact wording of the ownership clause or control agreement and on the laws of the state. Once joint ownership is established, the other person can act alone at any time, whether you are ill or not. And full ownership passes to the surviving party on the death of the other.

You can sign a document giving someone else the power to act for you. It can be limited or blanket authority. Like joint ownership or control, the other person has the right to act in the capacity to which he has been authorized at any time, whether you are sick or well.

A trust is another method to transfer legal title to a portion or all of your assets to another person specifically to be

133

used for your benefit. An arrangement of this sort is based on a trust agreement signed by you and the trustee. This document sets forth the manner in which you want your property used and its disposition at the time of your death.

Trusts are often used by people who have substantial amounts of property, usually with a bank or trust company acting as trustee. Trusts can also be used by people of moderate means if they can find someone who is willing to act as trustee for them, either free of charge or for a small fee.

Pick someone in whom you have complete confidence. He or she must be meticulously honest and should be capable of managing any of your business affairs. He should also have good judgment about the kind of care you need, know how to provide it, and have your best interest at heart.

A good personal friend or a trusted relative is often the best agent you can find. But don't choose a family member simply because you feel obligated to do so. In this of all things, consider your interests first.

Some agencies are willing to accept this responsibility for older people who do not have close friends or relatives. Your local health and welfare council or the public welfare department can usually recommend an agency in your community.

Your banker or lawyer is probably qualified to manage your business affairs. And by consulting with your doctor and others, he can make plans for you and your household as well. But professional people do not undertake this sort of responsibility unless they are well paid for their services. Be certin you agree in advance on fees, and find out whether you can cancel the agreement without penalty.

CONSUMER FRAUD

Unfortunately, retirees are likely and lucrative targets for many swindlers who gain their confidence and, eventually, their bankrolls. When it comes to protecting yourself in retirement, you can't be too careful.

The swindles that are aimed directly at America's retired population are so prevalent that a special hearing on the subject was held by the House Select Committee on Aging.

James Bolte, a New York City police officer, told the committee how retirees have been bilked by signing phony contracts, paying plumbers who never showed up to do the work and signing for a free termite inspection only to pay the "inspectors" hundreds of dollars to fix imaginary structural problems.

The elderly are also singled out for the "bank examiner" confidence game. It works like this: A con man disguised as a policeman or bank officer tells the victim that there have been suspicious withdrawals at the bank. The victim is asked to cooperate in apprehending the suspected thief by withdrawing some or all of his own money and turning it over to the con man. The victim is told that the money will be redeposited shortly in a special account that the bank can monitor. But when the victim returns to the bank, he finds that his money is gone and the phony bank examiner has fled.

"These are crimes which result in profound and very real human suffering," one committee member said. "The elderly person who loses his entire life saving endures a trauma so severe that his only recourse is to isolate himself in his home to live out the rest of his life in desperate poverty and loneliness. For the victim who suffers an act of violence, their problems are compounded by the fact that they are likely not to recover from the injuries inflicted."

WHY RETIREES ARE TARGETS

John Murphy, acting commander of New York City's pickpocket and confidence squad, said that he believes retirees get taken because they are lonely. There is generally a promise of some fast money to be made in any type of con game, but Murphy doesn't think greed is what motivates the retirees who fall for the swindles. On the surface, many of the confidence games seem silly, but they are pulled off by polished performers.

How do you go about protecting yourself from such a swindle? Murphy gives this advice: "If you meet somebody on the street and if they found money and they are going to share it with you or if they want you to go to the bank and take out money of your own to show good faith, or if a man says he is a policeman and wants you to go to the bank and take out money to help him make an arrest, do not do it. Never take money out of the bank for anybody. No policeman is going to ask you to take funds out of a bank."

Murphy said that when a younger person falls for some sort of a confidence game he hardly ever loses less than several hundred dollars. But when the confidence game is worked against retirees, the victims often lose thousands of dollars, even their life savings. Out of twenty-five cases he selected at random, fifteen turned out to involve victims over fifty-five years old. The total amount of money lost by those under fifty-five was $7,700; for those over fifty-five the amount was $89,000.

The elderly are also more vulnerable to consumer fraud. Miracle hearing aids, machines to cure cancer and the like do a booming business. Other frequent ploys are social or travel clubs that require the applicant to sign contracts obligating them to long-term payments. A retiree who loses money in such schemes suffers all the more because his earning power is gone and his chances of recouping are meager.

You can't be completely protected against crime, but knowing how criminals operate can make you a less-likely target. The New York Police Department urges, for example, that you break long-standing predictable habits. For example, if you are in the habit of going for a walk at one o'clock every afternoon, begin to stagger the time so that a burglar or mugger won't be able to predict your moves. And, the department says, be wary of any kind of "get-rich" scheme. In New York, confidence games are often operated by women, so don't be duped simply because you are approached by a pleasant, well-dressed woman.

The best defense against consumer fraud or outright swindles is to be skeptical. Beware of miracle cures, and don't sign anything obligating you to long-term payments without first having it checked by a lawyer. Better to be safe than sorry.

Chapter 12

Senior Power and the Future

By sheer strength of numbers, older Americans represent a powerful—and growing—political force in the U.S. A recent Census Bureau report showed that if present birthrates continue, over 17 percent of the population will be sixty-five or older by the year 2030, compared with 10.5 percent today and only 4 percent in 1900. The report further noted that between 1960 and 1970, the over-sixty-five population increased by 20 percent, while the population as a whole grew by 13 percent. The big rise in the percentage of the population over sixty-five is expected to come between 2010 and 2020, when the post-World War II baby boom passes sixty-five.

The political implications of this trend are enormous. Until the last decade, politicians paid little attention to older Americans because their numbers were fewer and they were disorganized and splintered. Now there are numerous organizations speaking and agitating on behalf of a healthier, better-educated retiree population, and they are making their voices heard—loudly. Groups such as the Gray Panthers, the American Association of Retired Persons, Retired Teachers of America and many others are pushing for "senior power," and they are getting it.

The senior-citizen lobby in Washington helped create the pressure that resulted in the passage of Medicare and an increase in Social Security benefits seven times in little more than a decade. Thanks partly to the efforts of senior lobbies, food stamps have been made available to the low-income elderly, the National Nutrition Program was enacted, and millions of dollars in federal funds have been allocated to help identify and solve the problems of retirees.

137

POWER OF THE VOTE

Political leaders are listening to the demands made by retirees partly because studies show that they get out and vote. And when all of the organizations representing retirees— or those nearing retirement—unite, the voting bloc can total several million.

The Census Bureau conducted a survey in 1975 showing that of the 63 million Americans who voted in congressional elections, one out of every three votes was cast by someone over age sixty-five. Fifty-eight percent of those between the ages of fifty-five and sixty-five voted—a much higher rate than for any other age group.

An official with the Administration on Aging in Washington has said that "babies are out and old folks are in." Indeed, retirees are showing increasing influence on politics on a national, state and local level.

The degree of their strength was demonstrated nationally during the 1964 presidential campaign. The Republican candidate, Sen. Barry Goldwater, suggested publicly that Social Security should be made voluntary. His opponent, President Lyndon Johnson, seized on the issue, airing televised campaign messages showing a pair of hands ripping a Social Security card in half. The elderly vote swung to Johnson, even in traditionally Republican areas such as St. Petersburg, Fla.

Similarly, retirees in Florida, who number more than 1.5 million, have kept politicians fighting against increases in electricity rates there. In 1975, the state's Public Service Commission turned down a $14.5 million rate-rise request by an electrical utility, largely because of pressure from retirees.

The 34,000 residents of Sun City, Ariz., a retirement community, united in 1970 to defeat a proposal to raise school taxes. The county board of supervisors finally created a special district, excluding Sun City, so that taxes could be increased without affecting the retirees. Elderly voters in Monmouth County, N.J., were credited with defeating a similar school-funding proposal there in 1974.

In places such as Miami Beach, Fla., where large concentrations of retirees live, senior citizens have the most influential political voice of all. Bobby Goodman, a former city councilman, was voted out of office in 1975 when he went on record opposing programs that the retirees supported.

A report to the Senate Select Committee on Aging says that most of the legislation concerning the elderly has been passed in 10 states: California, Florida, Illinois, Massachusetts, Michigan, New Jersey, New York, Ohio, Pennsylvania and Texas. In all these states, retirees make up a large portion of the population.

William R. Hutton, executive director of the National Council of Senior Citizens, one of the most influential retiree organizations, recalls that not too many years ago retiree lobbyists were given a hasty brush-off by elected officials. "We would wait for hours in hopes the legislator would pass through and we could plead our case in a quick standing visit or fast walk down the hall." That's all changed now, he says. "While all of Congress is surely not beating a path to our door, it is uniquely satisfying to hear from legislators via letters and telephone visits—asking how we stand on issues, asking how a certain proposal or piece of legislation might affect the elderly, asking for advice."

INTERNSHIP PROGRAM

The House of Representatives, recognizing the increasing political activity and strength of retirees, has developed a Senior Citizen Internship program to help familiarize them with the legislative process. Usually, each congressional office will have two senior interns at a time, often a husband-and-wife team. They are paid a small stipend while they are enrolled in the program.

Mr. and Mrs. Cyril Kidgell of Ohio spent two weeks as interns for Rep. Ralph Regula. Up to that time, they hadn't known how Congress operated. "We learned about the programs being proposed for helping the older American," they

139

wrote in a report, "and were able to come home and inform
the members of several senior groups about our experiences
and acquaint them with various bills being considered in Congress for their benefit."

Mr. and Mrs. Paul Peridue of Anderson, Ind., returned
home after one week as interns in Washington and toured the
state telling senior-citizen councils how they could lobby to
get legislation enacted.

The senior-citizen intern program benefits congressmen,
too. The interns often come away from Washington impressed
with their elected leaders. They no longer feel so totally al-
ienated from the legislative process that governs their lives.

Though elderly voters are increasingly marshaling their
strength at the polls, issues of concern to this expanding and
increasingly potent group remain.

Dr. Butler, the author of "Why Survive? Growing Old in
America," told the House Select Committee on Aging that
what older Americans want most is independence.

"That independence has to be realistic," he said. "It
doesn't mean living under shabby, penurious circumstances,
malnourished and uncomfortable. It does mean being able to
remain in your own home if you basically have the capacity
to do so," even though, he said, people might need assistance
to make it possible.

To be independent, retirees must be given the right to
work and earn enough money to live decently without jeopardizing their Social Security payments. Numerous groups
have recommended that the Social Security earning ceiling
be lifted entirely, as it is for those over seventy-two. Others
say that retirees should be allowed to earn at least $7,500 a
year without affecting their Social Security benefits.

"The question of income for older people is a top priority,"
Donald F. Reilly, deputy commissioner of the Administration
on Aging told a congressional committee. "If you solve that
problem, you can solve a lot of other problems."

Many retirees want a "right to work" law that will not
force them into mandatory retirement. "It makes no social

sense for us not to allow older people to work and support themselves when able," Dr. Butler said. "Indeed, we should encourage people who have the capacity, the desire and need to continue to work."

COUNCIL'S PRIORITIES

The National Council on Aging (NCOA), is working to help isolate the problems of older Americans and to recommend solutions. One of its affiliates, the National Media Resource Center on Aging, sponsored a Louis Harris poll of American attitudes toward aging. The poll found that 81 percent believe that the government should help support older people with taxes collected from all Americans, and 67 percent believe that no matter how little a person earned during his working years, he should have enough to live on when he is retired.

NCOA made specific recommendations for legislative remedies to the problems of aging in this country:

RETIREMENT: Flexible retirement ages should be adopted by employers and unions, allowing those who wish to do so to retire early or at the "normal" retirement age of sixty-five, and others should be allowed to work as long as they are able. A comprehensive physical examination should be the determining factor as to whether a worker can continue to hold a job after age sixty-five.

EMPLOYMENT SERVICE: The Manpower Administration should appoint full-time specialists who would work at the state and local level to place older workers in jobs. A financial-incentive program should be established to reward companies that hired older workers. The Manpower Administration should create a pilot employment service aimed at finding jobs, for workers over forty.

SENIOR COMMUNITY SERVICE PROJECTS: These would be similar to the senior centers that are already functioning across the nation. They would have the additional responsibility of finding work for older people and helping them become involved in community projects.

PRE-RETIREMENT PLANNING: Pre-retirement counseling should be established on the job to reduce the mistakes and frustrations that accompany a "trial and error" approach to retirement. "The federal government should recognize the need for planning and assume a partnership with educational institutions and private industry by funding research and training programs, sponsoring projects, and providing incentives for employers to pay the tuition for appropriate courses, as well as setting an example as a model employer," NCOA says.

SECOND CAREERS: Career-oriented educational and training programs should help persons transfer from one field to another.

WOMEN AND MINORITIES: Because they often suffer most from unemployment and economic deprivation during retirement, single women and members of minority groups should be given special consideration.

Retirees seem assured of an increasing voice in political affairs of the nation, and greater participation in the mainstream of American life. A major consulting firm has urged U.S. industry to start gearing itself toward manufacturing goods for an older population. Older Americans are going to have more to spend and a stronger say in what happens in the nation.

President Herbert Hoover once said. "Our civilization's future will not depend upon what man does on the job, but what he does in his life off the job." With the promise of better health, increased longevity and the financial means to live comfortably, the retirement years can be ones to look forward to.

Chapter 13

Four Success Stories

"I'm dead against it," Col. Harland Sanders said about mandatory retirement in testimony to the House Select Committee on Aging. Sanders, eighty-six, noted that he was sixty-six when he began the fried-chicken franchising business that made him a millionaire.

Similar views about retirement were expressed by actress Ruth Gordon, eighty; Washington lawyer Tommy Corcoran, seventy-six, and U.S. Commissioner on Aging Dr. Arthur Flemming, seventy-one.

Surprisingly, however, Sen. S. I. Hayakawa, seventy, advocated forced retirement. The retired college president explained that compulsory retirement makes people try something new. "You need something in life to tell you to move on," he said.

Of course, Hayakawa moved on to the Senate. Yet, the issue of retirement is a very subjective thing. It is paradoxical that at the very time the debate on compulsory retirement was boiling up in Congress, more and more workers in certain industries were opting to take early retirement. Some people adjust easily to the idea; others just can't accept it. Some people "move on" to new jobs; others move on to a life of ease—or a life of bitterness. It's largely a matter of adjustment.

Here are the stories of four people who have made the adjustment successfully—and how they did it.

143

CHILLY HARNER

At seventy-five, Charles E. (Chilly) Harner is beginning a new career.

Being associate editor of a business magazine wasn't keeping him busy enough, so Harner accepted a job editing a weekly newspaper. It is located just a few blocks from his pleasant waterfront home in Sarasota, Fla., and he can walk to work if he wants to.

"I don't know what it would be like to retire," Harner said, relaxing at tea time with his wife, Sherry. "I've never tried it for very long."

Harner stands six feet, two inches tall and is lean and muscular. There is still a spring in his step when he takes his long walk every morning, and his deep voice is firm.

"We've seen a lot of retired people who have become alcoholics because they have nothing else to do," Harner says. "The priest of our church said that was one of his main worries. Two-thirds of the parishioners were retired and a lot of them are drunk all the time. They get bored with life, so they take up drinking as a crutch."

Today, Harner and his wife prefer tea to martinis, but that wasn't always the case. He worked in Chicago as a newspaper editor and on the staff of the Associated Press until he was forty-one. Both were high-pressure jobs. "I would get so sick of the pressure that I had to have two or three martinis every night before I could eat," Harner recalls. "Then my wife and I discovered that it didn't agree with us as we got older. Once it started to unsettle us, we stopped drinking."

During World War II, Harner joined the Army Air Corps as a captain. His eyes were so bad that he had to get a special waiver before they would admit him. In fact, he had difficulty passing the physical examination, and a doctor ordered him to stop smoking.

"I was a very heavy cigarette smoker, but I stopped smoking at 4 p.m. on May 8, 1944, and I haven't had a cigarette since," Harner said. "The first three days I thought I was going to die. But I think it's one of the reasons that I feel as good as I do these days."

When he left the Associated Press after fourteen years, he collected a grand total of $76. "The Associated Press started the pension program just a couple of months before I quit," Harner says. "In those days you didn't think about getting a pension. You just kept on working as long as you could."

Harner and his wife developed an interest in fishing and decided one day to move to California. They opened a small public relations and advertising business, spending most of their free time fishing. When he was fifty-one, a friend with the State Department in Washington persuaded him to help form the U.S. Information Agency. Harner joined the State Department and spent twelve years in Latin American as a public-relations consultant.

"I had thought about retirement before, but that's the first time I thought about getting a pension," Harner recalls. "I went into the agency at fifty-one and came out when I was sixty-three. We never thought about having a guaranteed income.

"Sherry and I have had a very good life," he says. "The idea was to live while we were living, so we never really gave much thought about tomorrow. We didn't put much aside the way people should. When I came out of the Foreign Service, there was an annuity and I was also eligible for Social Security, but I didn't take it."

Harner had managed to invest in a few stocks. His State Department annuity, together with the dividend income from the stocks, allowed them to retire to the Florida Keys and buy a house in the small town of Marathon.

"We were going to spend the rest of our lives fishing," Harner recalls. "But that didn't last very long. We got bored. After three months, we quit fishing, and after three more months, we quit eating fish."

Sleepy little Marathon didn't offer them much once the enticement of fishing was gone. Harner had been very busy

145

all of his life, and at sixty-four, he was still healthy and ready for excitement. Through a former associate, he got a job editing a new business magazine in Tampa.

"I enjoyed that job tremendously," Harner recalls. "I stayed there for five years and watched the magazine grow into a first-class publication. I found that being editor was getting to be pretty tough so I resigned just before I was seventy."

Harner is still associate editor of the magazine and does special assignments. Occasionally, he writes stories for other magazines.

Typically, Harner soon became restless without a regular job. So when he was offered the editorship of the weekly newspaper, he jumped at the chance. He goes to work every day, returning home by four o'clock in the afternoon to have tea with his wife.

"I think these little breaks are tremendously important," Harner says. "We enjoy tea as much as we used to enjoy cocktails. We really look forward to four o'clock."

Harner shows no signs of slowing down. He believes that his active life and interests—and his firm religious beliefs—are responsible for his good health and happiness.

"I think that if you stopped you'd just go downhill and get sick," Harner says. "I don't believe you can work hard all of your life and then fold up your wings and expect to be happy. If you do that, you might just as well stop living."

What is Harner's secret? Part of it is a natural inclination toward good health and a long life, but he also takes good care of himself. He gets a good night's sleep every night and a nap in the afternoon lasting anywhere from 15 minutes to two hours. Both he and his wife watch what they eat and get regular exercise.

"Sherry is an excellent cook and she makes sure we have a balanced diet," Harner says. "I keep my weight between 168 and 171. We don't eat much fat, watch the meat, and restrict our carbohydrates. It makes a big difference in how we feel."

Until he reached his seventy-fourth birthday, Harner jogged five miles every morning. He has recently slowed down to a brisk walk. "It's very quiet in the early morning," he says. "I wake up and I can hardly wait to get out there and start walking." For Harner, retirement is simply a phase of life that has been filled with both work and pleasure. He is doing the same things today that he has done most of his life, in spite of the fact that he is eligible for Medicare, Social Security and a government pension.

"I don't intend to slow down," Harner says. "Why should I? I feel wonderful and I absolutely love life. Who knows, maybe there's another career waiting for me after this newspaper-editing job."

CHARLES BUSH

Retirement came to Charles Bush unexpectedly. He developed cataracts in both eyes and had to have surgery. The operation left him incapacitated and bedridden for a year, and he was forced to resign from his job as school superintendent of Clark County, Ill., at age sixty-two.

The cataract operation disrupted all his careful retirement plans. He had intended to work as school superintendent until age sixty-five, and then take an administrative job with the athletic department at Indiana State University, where he once played football.

"The truth is that I wouldn't really be retired if it hadn't been for my eyesight," he says. "I planned on working at the university because I love athletics, and I wanted to do some teaching and help recruit students."

The year flat on his back left him out of shape, but you'd never know it now. He is a trim, energetic man with wavy gray hair, an elfin face and a booming voice. His fitness was no accident. "Exercise is one of the most important things that anybody can do, especially when they're getting older," he says. "I've always exercised every day, and when I was unable to do it for a year, I really fell apart. I had to work a long time to get the old body back in shape."

147

His vision is poor because he needs additional surgery on the lens of one eye. But he says he is happy in retirement.

"It came about unexpectedly, but we have adjusted to it," he says. "I'm getting involved in things again, and that's important. I've always been into things, you know, so I don't see how I can change that. You don't change when you retire, you just become more yourself, whether it's good or bad. You have more time to do the same things you always did."

For most of the 20 years he has lived there, Bush has been one of the leading citizens in Marshall, Ill., a slow-paced county seat (pop. 3,200) in an agricultural area. Much of his spare time has been spent working to provide more recreation facilities in the town.

The first project he spearheaded was raising several thousand dollars to build an American Legion hall and to serve as the center of social activities for young and old alike. Then he led a drive to raise $85,000 for a community swimming pool. A county fairgrounds was constructed under his leadership and, just before his cataract operation, he helped raise money to construct a nursing home that cost nearly $1 million.

"I really believe that every kind of experience you have in dealing with people and bettering your community is going to be helpful to you in retirement," he says. "I think being happy in retirement is a matter of going outside of yourself to help others. Good will is one of the few things you have to give away in order to keep."

Reflecting on how he was able to bounce back so quickly after his long illness, Bush says, "I believe you have to be very much involved with things outside of yourself and your work, and I think you have to have a deep spiritual commitment. My wife and I have always been very active in the community and our church and we still are. I believe that spirituality is what gives us both the energy and sense of well-being that we enjoy."

Bush's wife, Mildred, a former teacher in the Clark County school system, retired when her husband was forced to leave his job. She says she thought it would be a blow to his ego if she worked when he didn't. Besides, they both have good pensions and he draws full Social Security because of his disability. They have no financial problems, having long since paid off their mortgage and most of their debts.

"Financial planning is terribly important," Bush says. "You simply can't do enough of it. But I don't think it's as important as a feeling of being worth something as a human being. All the money in the world won't help if you're unhappy with yourself and life in general."

Since his recovery, Bush has donated much time to Indiana State University, where he has been president of the Varsity Club, the alumni association and several other organizations. He is helping raise money for scholarships and recruiting students.

Bush's life is really not much different than when he was working. The telephone jangles constantly and he races to it, dispensing advice in a hearty baritone. Will he be available to help out with this project? Of course he will. Now, I don't want to tell you what to do, but if I were you. . . .

Both of their children live in Marshall and teach at Indiana State University. There are four grandchildren who consider the Bushes' big, yellow and white Georgian home a warm family gathering place. It is the homestead that three generations enjoy.

There is no such thing as a typical day at the Bush home except on Sunday. Then they go to church, have the noon meal out, and perhaps have guests or their children and grandchildren home for the evening meal. During the week, they may go out to eat two or three times, and they often entertain at home. They have kept this schedule for years.

"Even when I'm at home, I stay busy," Bush says. "I always have helped Mildred around the house, but now I can do more, so I do. She deserves a break, too. Let me tell you, respect between a man and a wife is tremendously important. When you get older and your sex drive starts to diminish— and it will, believe me—you have to have something else going for you. We don't waste time brooding about things we wish we could do. We go out and do all of the things that we can."

Mildred has given piano lessons to children for years. Their lives have changed little in retirement, except that they have more freedom. Sometimes this freedom makes retirees feel at loose ends. What is the Bushes' secret?

"I believe that you're going to be the same kind of person in retirement that you were all of your life," Bush says. "I think you have to work hard to develop other interests outside of your job. You have to learn to respect yourself before you can get the respect of other people. The only way you can build that respect is by getting out and doing things for others. When you start thinking too much about yourself, you've had it. Especially when you retire, because, brother, you'll have a lot of time on your hands to sit around and feel miserable."

JOHN BAXTER

Retiring early from a hectic supervisory job that kept him traveling 80 percent of the time was no great trauma for John Baxter, who used to wonder how he was going to spend his time once he retired. Now that he has been retired for several years, he only wishes he had done it earlier.

Operating out of an office in New Jersey, Baxter was regional sales manager for a large Midwestern concern, supervising nearly 150 managers and salesmen for the company's industrial division in the eastern United States.

In 1970, at age sixty, Baxter and his wife decided that they had had enough of work. They had been thinking about retirement for several years, but were surprised to discover one day that they had automatically begun to make plans for the transition.

"The idea of retirement just grew on us," Baxter recalls. "We knew that someday we were going to retire. I suppose we were making casual plans without even thinking about it. I don't miss work at all, but I still have some connection with it. It isn't a big one, but it's enough to make me feel as if I'm still part of the company. That means a lot to me."

Baxter has had more good fortune than most retirees. He is blessed with good health, a bright outlook on life, and a general sense of well-being. His wife also had an inheritance that included two small oil wells.

Baxter, who used to travel almost constantly, stay out late for business meetings, and write long memorandums to his subordinates, now lounges quietly at home in Sarasota, Fla., and listens to the fish jump in the canal just beyond his swimming pool.

Baxter and his wife live in a small development called Siesta Isles, on a small island. They were among the first residents of their community and had few friends in the area. The move to Florida was prompted more by instinct than anything else.

"We had no really close friends here," Baxter says. "And we didn't know much about the area. We had spent a good deal of time looking at model houses around St. Petersburg and Clearwater on some of our visits, but we seemed to gravitate to Sarasota." They picked out a lot and built a new house, using a plan they helped design.

On their earlier trips to Florida, the Baxters were turned off by the activities they saw older people involved in. Shuffleboard seemed too tame for them.

"I thought the older people looked depressed at first," Baxter says. "The picture changed year after year. Finally, we decided that the retirees were doing exactly the same kinds of things that we wanted to do. Your perspective changes as you get older."

Baxter is a strong, robust man who is always puttering with something, although he has no particular hobby to dominate his time. He and his wife spend long hours each week mowing, trimming and sprucing up the yard. Aside from the yard, there is the routine housework, a little maintenance and cleaning the swimming pool.

"We know some people who live for golf," Baxter says.

151

"We don't have any one thing to consume us. We see different groups to add variety to our lives. Seeing the same people over and over again is a mistake because you get in a rut."

A typical day begins at 6 a.m. with coffee and the newspaper. Then there might be a quick dip in the heated pool, a trip around the yard to pull weeds, or just lazing around the patio listening to the birds sing and the mullet jumping in the canal. Lunch is around noon, consisting of a bottle of beer, a sandwich, and a glass of milk. That is followed by a short nap, with dinner whenever they get around to it.

"We don't schedule our lives," Baxter says. "We're retired and don't want to be regimented anymore. We do what we want to do whenever we want to do it. I don't seem to have a lot of things to do, but I don't know where the time goes."

Only rarely does he reflect on his working career.

"I wake up at night sometimes and think about it," he muses. "I wonder what I might be doing now if I still worked there. You can't spend 34 years on a job without having it grow on you."

The transition from work to leisure was a natural one for him. Baxter never shuffled papers at home. Work stayed in his office. Home was always a sanctuary, a place for leisure activities. So in retirement, the home remains what it always has been to him.

Days of having nothing to do don't make him feel guilty. Neighbors drive by and he calls to them by name when he's in the yard. They stop and chat, then go about their business. He loves Florida weather, and the summer heat and humidity don't bother him.

Fortunately, the Baxters have no financial worries. He had a good pension plan and began exercising stock options years ago. When he reached age sixty, he had a good idea what his retirement income would be. It was considerably lower than when he was working, but then oil was discovered on the farm his wife had inherited.

The Baxters have never kept a precise budget, but they have always been conservative with their money. They pay cash for even big purchases. When they sold their home in New Jersey, they used the money to build their retirement home.

"We were among the fortunate," Baxter admits. "My wife used to worry about whether or not we would have enough to live on when we retired. She was looking ahead, but who can tell what inflation is going to do? Both of us worried about it a great deal."

Baxter knew that they could retire at age sixty without lowering their standard of living. After he arrived at that decision, he began preparing the way for retirement.

He told his superiors six months ahead of time when he would be retiring. Then he talked with the personnel officer to find out all he needed to know about benefits such as medical and life insurance. He found out how much he would receive from his pension, when he would get it, who administered the fund and to whom he should complain if there were problems.

"We examined things very carefully," says Baxter. "I had an idea about how much I would be making if I stayed with the company until I was sixty-five, and we knew how much I would have if I retired at age sixty. We also knew that I probably wouldn't advance in the company because I didn't want to move to the home office. After we had all the information, we decided to hell with it. So here we are."

Some people feel an immediate euphoria in the early days of retirement, followed by depression when the permanence of their situation strikes home. With Baxter, the euphoria hit and stayed.

"I'm happier now than I was when I was working," he says. "Physically, I feel much better because I'm not being pushed all the time. I don't let inflation or anything else worry me, because I can't do anything about it. Everything will work out because it always does."

Actually, Baxter thinks the change to retirement is more difficult for women than for most men. A man, he says, is always out in the world doing different things, going places,

153

and talking with different people. But a wife's world revolves around a smaller circle of friends.

"She develops a lot of close social contacts," he says. "It's harder for her to give those up than it is for a man to leave his world because he isn't as personally involved in it."

Baxter's wife became active in several social organizations in Sarasota and, before long, both had found many new friends. They never get lonely from lack of a social life.

Inflation has sent the cost of living soaring in the years since they retired, but his stock has gone up and split, paying a dividend that helps compensate for the increased living expenses. When he was sixty-two, he and his wife both opted for early Social Security benefits, increasing their nontaxable income by a little more than $300 a month. If they had been forced to live only on his pension and Social Security, they would have had to lower their standard of living considerably.

"We could get by," he says, "but we certainly couldn't live in the house we have, in the area we're in, and we couldn't drive a Cadillac."

All the money in the world won't make life pleasant if you are unhealthy, Baxter says, but even if you have good health, your retirement can be a nightmare if you don't have enough money.

What is his formula for a happy retirement? It includes financial planning, relaxation, not taking yourself too seriously, and accepting retirement as a natural stage of life, not a disaster.

"Retirement is a challenge," he says. "It's another phase of life to enjoy if you don't worry too much about it. You have to accept the fact that you're a retiree, but you don't have to sit around feeling sorry for yourself. Don't think, 'I'm going to die tomorrow.' That'll get you down. What you have to do is think about living and enjoy it. Personally, I wish I had retired 50 years earlier."

VIRGINIA KUNZIC

Stanley and Virginia Kunzic, bundled warmly to protect themselves from the crisp Colorado mountain air, arrive back at their home in Buena Vista after catching three lake trout. They had to chop a hole in the ice before they could drop in their lines.

"Oh, Lord, I missed this invigorating cool weather and the mountain trout," Virginia says. "It's so good to be back here."

The Kunzics broke the usual pattern and moved away from Florida's warm climate to retire in Colorado.

"It was a joint decision," Virginia says. "Both of us love Colorado and never particularly cared for Florida."

Virginia, who retired in 1975 after having worked as an office manager for a high-pressure college fund-raising operation, reflects on the pleasures of the quiet life.

"Maybe the mountain air has cooled my blood," she says, sighing. "I don't miss the work at all. In fact, I've never been so glad to be out of anything in my life. I miss some of the people I worked with once in awhile, but it's a rare day that I ever think about the job."

Stanley and Virginia had planned for several years to retire to Buena Vista and, two years before they did, they purchased a two-bedroom house and rented it to tenants. When the time came to retire, they were all set to go. They simply loaded the things they would need on a truck and took off.

"We had planned everything so carefully that it was just like going down to the drugstore to get a bottle of aspirin," Virginia says. "I kept working long enough to get enough quarters to eventually qualify for Social Security. I also wanted to wait for Stanley to get tired of his job. When he quit, I quit. And, brother, this is the life."

Viriginia is only fifty-five, so she doesn't receive a Social Security benefit, and she doesn't have a private pension. Stanley is a retired Army sergeant, and they live on his Army pension and Social Security benefits. When they were in Florida, Stanley worked as a printing supervisor for a chamber of commerce. When they retired, their income was cut in half.

"It isn't any trouble," Virginia says. "You simply adjust to your new way of life. We eat just as well as we ever did and we have everything that we want. We don't go out quite as often to spend money, but we have other things to enjoy that don't cost much. Before, it was no big thing if we wanted to blow a couple of hundred dollars on a weekend. We don't do that now, but we don't miss it."

There are other savings: They don't spend as much on clothing now, the utilities in Buena Vista cost much less than they did in Florida, and the small retirement home is cheaper to maintain.

"There was only one thing about retiring that ever bothered me," Virginia says. "I was afraid about Stanley and I both being in the same house 24 hours a day because we are both so active. I was afraid we would get under each other's skin. It's a small house, so we do get in each other's way once in a while, but we never get under each other's skin. There's a big difference."

Stanley helps out around the house so that his wife will have it easier. He dries the dishes, vacuums the house occasionally and cooks some of the meals. Most of his work, however, is with outside maintenance chores.

"When we get up in the morning, we hardly ever have definite plans," Virginia says. "We do just exactly what we want to do. If we feel like going to Colorado Springs, we go. Both of us love to fish, so we go to the mountains quite a bit to catch lake trout."

Stanley is able to buy their food and other household items cheaply from a nearly military commissary. They also receive free health care.

"I do a great deal of house cleaning," Virginia says. "I never get bored and I never—but never—miss my job. I believe the secret to a happy retirement is planning, spelled in capital letters. You have to know what you're going to have, what you can afford, where you want to live and how to cut back on things you can't afford to do anymore. You also have to adjust your physical and mental outlook and realize that there are limitations to what you can expect out of yourself when you're retired."

She thought for a moment and passed on another secret to a happy retirement. "You have to have a good husband who loves you and who you can love right back," she says. "That makes everything all right."

BIBLIOGRAPHY

A Brief Explanation of Medicare, U.S. Department of Health, Education and Welfare, Washington, D.C.

A Guide to Budgeting for the Family, U.S. Department of Agriculture, Washington, D.C.

A Guide to Budgeting for the Retired Couple, U.S. Department of Agriculture, Washington, D.C.

Aging in American Society, by James D. Manney Jr., Institute of Gerontology, University of Michigan, Ann Arbor, Mich.

The Aging Consumer, Institute of Gerontology, University of Michigan, Ann Arbor, Mich.

The Complete Guide to Retirement, by Thomas Collins, Prentice Hall, Englewood Cliffs, N.J.

The Condominium Book by Lee Butcher, Dow Jones Books, Princeton, N.J.

Consumer Income, U.S. Department of Commerce, Washington, D.C.

Developments in Aging, U.S. Government Printing Office, Washington, D.C.

Estimating Your Social Security Retirement Check, U.S. Department of Health, Education and Welfare, Washington, D.C.

Gray Power, Florida Trend magazine, Tampa, Fla.

How Much to Spend on a Home, Institute of Food and Agricultural Sciences, University of Florida, Gainesville, Fla.

How to Retire and Enjoy It, by Ray Giles, Fawcett Publications, New York, N.Y.

The National Directory of Retirement Residences: Best Places to Live When You Retire, by Noverre Musson, Frederick Fell Publishers Inc., New York, N.Y.

No Longer Young, The Older Woman in America, The Institute of Gerontology, University of Michigan, Ann Arbor, Mich.

Preparation for Retirement, by Woodrow W. Hunter, Institute of Gerontology, University of Michigan, Ann Arbor, Mich.

Senior Opportunities and Services, U.S. Government Printing Office, Washington, D.C.

Social Security Rulings, U.S. Department of Health, Education and Welfare, Washington, D.C.

Social and Economic Characteristics of the Older Population, U.S. Department of Commerce, Washington, D.C.

Supplemental Security Income for the Aged, Blind and Disabled, U.S. Department of Health, Education and Welfare, Washington, D.C.

Tax Benefits for Older Americans, Department of the Treasury, Internal Revenue Service, Washington, D.C.

Toward a National Policy on Aging, U.S. Government Printing Office, Washington, D.C.

U.S. Housing Developments for the Elderly, Office of Housing Programs and Housing Management, Department of Housing and Urban Development, Washington, D.C.

Where To Retire On A Small Income, by Norman D. Ford, Harian Publications, Greenlawn, N.Y.

Working With Older People, U.S. Government Printing Office, Washington, D.C.

You, the Law and Retirement, by Virginia Lehman, U.S. Government Printing Office, Washington, D.C.

You and Your Money, by Eliott Janeway, David McKay, New York, N.Y.

ADDITIONAL — Transcripts of hearings before the U.S. House and Senate Select Committees on Aging from 1974–1976